SELECTING & IMPLEMENTING

HR & PAYROLL SOFTWARE

A Practical Guide

DENIS W. BARNARD

2nd Edition
Copyright © 2019 Denis W. Barnard.
ISBN: 9781912315932
ePub ISBN: 9781912315925
Imprint: Stergiou Books Limited
Dublin, Ireland

ACKNOWLEDGEMENTS

My thanks are due to Cezanne HR and HRcomparison Ltd for permission to reproduce some specific material here. I would also like to thank the many HR and payroll software vendors for generously sharing their expertise with me over the years, and the industry in general for being such an interesting one in which to be involved.

ABOUT THE AUTHOR

Denis Barnard is a consultant specialising in the selection of HR & payroll systems, and other HRIS, and is acknowledged as one of the UK's leading figures in the field.

In 1980, he moved from Finance to HR function and in 1984 began his association with software when his then employers asked him to computerise the manual payroll. Two years later, he did the same for the HR data, and has been involved in this aspect of HR ever since.

Over the years he has worked in a broad range of sectors, Local Government, Higher and Further Education, Music, Media, Technology, Manufacturing, Brewing and Retail to name just a few.

In 2009, he founded and launched the website **GPAcomparison** which at the time was the only site of its kind in the UK dedicated solely to HR & payroll software, and is still the source of choice for organisations and practitioners looking for systems information.

Apart from his consultancy work, Denis spends a significant amount of time producing articles, webinars, and seminars on HRIS topics. He is a director of the niche HRmeansbusiness consultancy and a contributor at **Global Talent Advisors**.

He is a keen naturalist and horticulturist in such spare time as can find.

CONTENTS

Introduction   11

Chapter 1 - Background   13

Chapter 2 - About HR Software   17

Chapter 3 - Project Preliminaries   32

Chapter 4 - "How Owns the Software?"   39

Chapter 5 - Making the Business Case   41

Chapter 6 - The Project Initiation Document   51

Chapter 7 - Immediate Activity 1   52

Chapter 8 - Immediate Activity 2   55

Chapter 9 - Immediate Activity 3   63

Chapter 10 - The Product Specification   68

Chapter 11 - Finding Vendors   74

Chapter 12 - Tendering   78

Chapter 13 - The Selection Process   92

Chapter 14 - The Decision   103

Chapter 15 - The Project Plan   108

Chapter 16 - Configuration   111

Chapter 17 - International   134

Chapter 18 - The New Software   139

Chapter 19 - Things That Can Go Wrong   146

Chapter 20 - Endgame   154

GLOSSARY   157

APPENDICES   174

Appendix One - Sample Hybrid Tender Document   175

Appendix Two - Sample Process Map - Leaver   199

Appendix Three - Supplier Demonstrations – Sample Scenarios   200

Appendix Four - The Big Five Benefits of an HR System   202

FIGURES

Fig. 1: Chapter 2 Summary Grid   30

Fig. 2: Data Flows Between the HRIS   31

Fig. 3: Project Stages   38

Fig. 4: Organisational Structure   56

Fig. 5: Posts and Conditions   57

Fig. 6: Posts and Benefits   58

Fig. 7: Grade-related Post Conditions   59

Fig. 8: Departmental Budget-to-Actuals   60

Fig. 9: Security Access Matrix   61

Fig. 10: Sample Starter Process   67

Fig. 11: Vendor Response Summary Sheet   89

Fig. 12: Costs of ownership of HRIS   91

Fig. 13: Demonstration Scoresheet   102

Fig. 14: Projected Timeline Plan   106

Fig. 15: Vendor Project Plan   110

Fig. 16: Triggered Action Example   118

Fig. 17: E-recruitment Work Flow   122

Fig. 18: Recruitment Administration Work Flow   123

Fig. 19: Gender Pay Gap Reporting 1   127

Fig. 20: Gender Pay Gap Reporting 2   127

Fig. 21: Chart Example   130

Fig. 22 Request for Replacement Hire Form   133

Fig. 23: International Matrix   135

Fig. 24: Starting Point for International Solution   136

Fig. 25: International Client Solution   137

Fig. 26: Bradford Factor Example   159

Fig. 27: Sample Leaver Process Map   199

.

INTRODUCTION

We are living through an era in which, thanks to the incessant demands of online journalism, HR is exhorted to take responsibility for everything from employee mental health to world peace. HR data analytics has its – largely uninformed - editorial supporters as well. The reason HR data has in reality not figured highly in management decision-making up to now has largely been due to the inaccuracy and lack of timeliness of such information as was available.

It has long been my contention that if there is one thing a good HR function should do for its employer organisation, it is to select, implement, and run an HR system which really works for all levels of that body. Here, at least, is a value-adding activity for practitioners to get their teeth into, and it's my experience that, up to now, we haven't done very well at it.

Choosing Human Resources and payroll software is an exercise in which nearly every HR and payroll practitioner will be involved at some point in their working lives; it can be one of the most time consuming and costly mistakes you ever make or, preferably, it could be extremely career-enhancing!

All too often, it's a case of "you don't know what you don't know", and there are horror stories everywhere!

In this book I have attempted to address the whole issue from start to finish – in understandable terms (perforce, because I can't write a line of code to save my life!) for people with only a very cursory acquaintance with this type of software – with a view to critically improving your chances of selecting the best fit for your requirements and then successfully rolling it out.

If there seems to be a rather heavier focus on the HR side of things, it is because HR systems can comprise many discrete modules in order to perform very differing tasks, whereas payroll software is geared towards the one all-important mission: take raw data, and pay and reward people in a compliant and timely manner.

Experience has shown me that there are two very clearly defined parts to this exercise: selecting the software, and then implementing it, each calling for a very particular skill set, and, most probably, two different teams.

The latter part of this book is aimed at giving the HR or payroll practitioner insight into what happens in the implementation phase. I don't expect for a moment that any of those practitioners will be physically managing this project (for reasons that will become clear later) but there will be a considerable amount of consultation on the configuration of your new software, and it will be a benefit to know what is actually going on in the background.

For those of you expecting me to name a "magic bullet" piece of software that solves all ills, I apologise in advance: there isn't one. The journey towards the right software begins with the client (you!) and your requirements. If you get that part right, the rest will follow.

When I first published this guide, the phenomena of artificial intelligence (AI) and chat bots had not burst upon the world of HR & payroll software. As yet, they are almost exclusively confined to the extremely large and expensive enterprise systems catering to global customers, but it follows that within a reasonable time frame they will be available to a wider range of customers.

The appeal of these features is fairly obvious, if only for organisations wishing to find themselves at the "leading edge of the digital world of HR". I have some reservations still about what this implies for purchasers; how much more they may need to pay, what in-house configuration expertise will be required in the future, and how these factors offset against the possible benefits, assuming that the purchasing organisation actually deploys them to maximum advantage. It could mean greater difficulty in changing over software suppliers. In addition, there is the issue of control over the AI "effect" and how to change it if it's not working as desired.

I have written at length about these dilemmas, talked to a number of players in the industry, and have yet to form a clear opinion on these extremely important points.

The good news at least is the basic methodologies and approach I describe in this book remain valid for the professional.

Denis W. Barnard

CHAPTER 1

BACKGROUND

> "I think we need a new HR system"

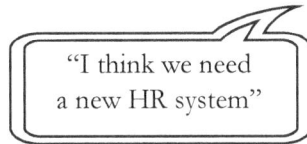

These words, delivered by the head of HR are guaranteed to provoke a variety of reactions from within the organisation: disbelief from the finance director who remembers the last bottomless money pit from the system bought 6 years ago; denial from the MD, who says we have one already; scepticism from other senior managers who remember the new information dawn that never seemed to materialise; and amusement from the payroll department, whose software is paying people very well, thank you, and change that over our dead bodies.

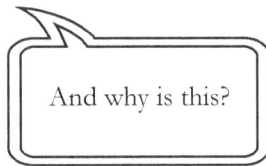

> And why is this?

The main reason is because of previous bad experiences; all of these projects started off initially with high optimism and great expectations, and finished off as partial successes, overspent budgets and no real visible benefits to the organisation.

The causes of this can lie in many directions, but it is usually down to a lethal cocktail of the buyer not really being very clear what they want and the supplier, wishing to make the sale, hoping that their application will ultimately do what the client thinks they want.

The fall-out is painful: tedious workarounds or double posting, sporadic and often inaccurate reporting resulting in demotivating frustration for all staff concerned and the attendant "bad press" within the organisation. What makes it worse is the fact that they are not getting the most value or functionality from their costly software, and continue to perform mundane administrative tasks that could easily have been done by the technology available.

These scenarios can often end with client and supplier falling out and new software being sought; however, unless the client is prepared to heed the lessons of history and take the correct steps next time around, they are preparing to repeat it with equally catastrophic consequences.

> So how do we re-write
> the story with
> a happy ending next
> time around?

Nothing in this world can guarantee success, but in our planning approach to this there are a number of critical steps that can be taken to radically minimise the chances of failure.

Firstly, then, let us consider some of the background to Human Resources Information Systems (HRIS for brevity).

HRIS is a generic term for any piece of software that captures or processes data relating to people in an organisation and facilitates access to this data for interpretation. The main and better-known examples of this are HR systems, payrolls, time and attendance applications and recruitment software. Nowadays, there is a lot of specialisation in the market place, so you can also acquire solutions to deal with absence, performance & appraisal, reward & benefits and learning & development.

Certainly until relatively recent times, personnel records were maintained on paper file or card systems, as also were payrolls. The latter were the first to become computerised, while the more viable computerised HR systems available were the preserve of the big players. In those days - the Eighties and early Nineties - to buy a system from a small software house was a gamble; either they could not sustain the support, or they just folded their tents and stole away. Many smaller organisations used – and continue to do so – spreadsheets, and other developed their own bespoke software.

Payroll software, by virtue of being the one source of who was actually employed and being paid, was relied upon for key management information such as headcount and salary budgets, although the actual data fields were geared more for pay, and not other important data such as development history and equal opportunity monitoring.

Large HR & payroll systems were, in the main, the responsibility of IT departments from a selection and ownership point of view, whilst the true sponsors of the software were relegated to the status of process operators; selection was based on IT suitability criteria (generally based around corporate IT philosophy, and compatibility with existing environments), and it was by no means unusual for all system administration and report writing to be channelled through IT for execution, a most unsatisfactory state of affairs and one that added no real value in real terms.

It is important to understand this state of affairs, as the focus on IT-led system selection and operation explains why there are still a large number of HR and payroll personnel who have at best, even now, a sketchy knowledge of these systems, how they work, and what they can do, which in turn has contributed to some very poor purchasing decisions over time.

During the Nineties, HR practitioners became aware of the advantages of more functional systems, and started to look for something better than spreadsheets, and reliable but unattractive DOS AS400 payroll systems started to look dated in the face of the Windows-based revolution.

Human Resources software has proceeded to accelerate its evolution over the past years, becoming more and more affordable as larger vendors and niche software houses take aim at the more populous sector of small- and medium-sized businesses, and developers concentrate on offering better configurability and user experience. Consequently, choice in the market place has grown for all types and sizes of organisations.

Apart from the increasing sophistication of organisational requirements for information, it must be said that another of the driving forces for change have really arisen from other types of software; people are used to intuitive software, easy configurability and rapid access which they use in their leisure time, such as that used on social platforms or gaming and utilities.

In-house servers have become unfashionable in the face of competition from vendor hosting, and IT intervention has rapidly become marginalised to the extent that their only function is to keep the broadband "pipe" running.

Currently, the industry is in a period of consolidation for some, and change for others. A spate of mergers and acquisitions in the HRIS market has subsided somewhat, while at the same time a whole new generation of applications is coming to market, some of which harness the power of smart phone "apps", others that are built on more powerful platforms. Systems are more affordable, prices are flexible and contracts are more negotiable, and more and more suppliers from around the world are entering the market place, increasing competition.

All these extra possibilities can cause a problem in themselves, with the prospective purchaser being overwhelmed by the sheer number of offerings. In the light of this, it is as important as ever to remain focused on finding the right software for you.

CHAPTER 2

ABOUT HR SOFTWARE

A typical comment from clients wishing to source HR & payroll software is that they "don't know what they don't know". In order to build a case for new software it is essential to understand the full range of functionality from these types of applications.

"We don't know what we don't know" really means that there is no accessible, complete and unbiased picture of what the software can do for them.

Certainly, they think they know what they want to achieve, but this overall perception often encounters a shortfall when taking into consideration the actual capabilities of the application. That is not to say that the software is deficient, it is rather that we as a profession don't really grasp what is going on inside it, and how it needs to be set up.

So that we can be talking on a level playing field with vendors and consultants, we need to appreciate the difference between **features** and **functions**.

A very succinct guide is this one:

"Functions are the "product's answer to the set of user tasks"; features are the "user tools" inherent in the product used to perform the functions" *(Wood, 1995).*

In the course of my work, I often use the analogy of how one goes about buying a car. If we apply the above definition, the function of a car is to get from A to B. For some there is additional required functionality, such as speed, fuel economy, comfort, price, public perception or off-road capability, or perhaps a combination of some of these.

To achieve these functions, features such as big engines, lightweight bodies, real hide seats, cheaper components, marque and four-wheel drive come into play.

This analogy goes part of the way to explain the past errors that have been made; the client's expectations of what would be delivered was a grand touring car, and the product, when it was switched on turned out to be a family hatchback!

It's a sad truth that even now I see requests on social media that run something like this:

"Can anyone recommend a really good HR system?"

Provoking a number of unqualified responses from vendors, resellers and a host of people who claim to have bought the right system.

I've often thought of running a question like "Can anyone recommend a good holiday destination?" just to see what the response is, and then to inform them that I'm partially incapacitated, love to lie in the sun or go shopping, and loathe long flights.

The value of the responses is not only negligible, but can be downright dangerous if they influence the purchase decision in any way.

So, the functions of an HR system can be said to be:

To provide a "single source of truth" for all employee and organisational information and to give access to this information in a way that enables the organisation to:

- manage performance
- recruit, track and develop talent
- reward to a competitive level
- reduce unnecessary absence
- identify trends across the workforce
- eliminate –or at least significantly reduce - manual administration by automating processes and actions.

The features that assist the product to fulfil these requirements are delivered on two levels, primarily in the various modules that comprise the software suite, and secondarily in the specific features within those modules.

HR software is nowadays usually integrated with payroll software and occasionally also with a time & attendance module. For now, we will focus on the HR-only element of the application, but the methodology approach is broadly the same" to "but the methodology and approach is broadly the same

A. HR software system modules

The core module of an HR system is the database, which will contain any number of pre-defined fields, and with the capacity to configure many more in various formats, e.g. alpha, numerical and alpha/numerical and field length. It is, in effect, a spreadsheet built to receive data.

This is the primary part to be populated in any implementation exercise, and these fields form the cornerstone of every action that is input or output from the application.

Structural data such as:

- Organisational and departmental set-up with locations and cost / profit centres; (see fig.4)
- Post hierarchies within departments;
- Job titles
- Post and grade attributes such as benefits, standard hours and full time equivalent (FTE) for headcount, etc.

Personal data:

- Names, addresses, telephone numbers
- Emergency contact
- Date of birth
- Gender, ethnic origin, other equality data
- Education level and achievements
- Work permits / visa

Job related personal data:

- Job title, department & grade
- Date joined (or date of continuous employment)
- Salary
- Rewards (bonuses and so on)
- Location
- Benefits

- Employment progression with organisation
- Training record
- Performance record.

Additional data:

- Fire officer / Certificate expiry
- Appointed persons
- Sports club membership

The exact nature and structure of all these data fields is one element of the configuration process with your vendor's project consultant, of which much more later.

The more usual modules that can be added to or integrated with the core database are:

Absence recording

The absence module collects and aggregates information on attendance, holidays and sickness. The main ways in which the module can be populated are by direct input from paper records, via a self service system or by upload from a Data Importer from an exterior source, such as a time & attendance application.

Absence modules facilitate use of the Bradford Factor method of evaluating sickness absence *(see Glossary)*

E-Learning or Learning management system (LMS)

This is a more advanced application than the conventional training administration module (q.v.).

A comprehensive LMS will pick up training and developmental needs from an employee appraisal (either from within the application or from a connected program) and track the whole process from gap analysis and needs identification, selection of materials, registration, delivery of electronic training and development materials and subsequent tracking.

With LMS, an organisation has considerable scope to bring together the various strands within learning & development, as they can range from induction, compliance renewals (e.g. First Aider Certificate), NVQs, and professional curricula all the way down to mentoring or observation.

Most integrated HR & payroll vendors do not offer an LMS; organisations requiring this will need to look for specialist vendors, and decide the point of confluence of the LMS with the main system.

E-Recruitment (also known as Applicant Tracking System – ATS)

E-recruitment modules will typically be used in connection with an organisation's own website recruitment page or job board. They work by streaming job applications (filtered if required) into the client's own self service system to any desired destination, be it the recruitment or HR department, or direct to the hiring manager.

The modules can be set up to manage the responses to applicants, and co-ordinate interview times, locations, and required interviewers.

The overall aim is to make a smoother recruitment experience for all parties concerned.

There are a number of HR & payroll software vendors who offer an e-recruitment module available to integrate with the HR & payroll suite and my advice would be to benchmark what they have to offer against that of some discrete modules offered by e-recruitment specialists.

(see also: Recruitment administration module)

Performance

Performance will cover the cycle from goal / target setting, periodic appraisal and measuring of progress towards the targets, and final results for (usually) the year, which may link to a multiplier, for instance, that auto-calculates the reward element of an employee's remuneration package.

Although performance may identify gaps or developmental actions needed to meet the targets, the delivery of these is normally carries out through either the e-Learning or training administration modules.

Recruitment administration

The recruitment administration module is another way of managing recruitment processes, but is far more labour intensive in nature.

Applications are logged, and responses run from templated documents by mail merges. Interview dates also need to be logged in the first instance.

There is a lot more manual intervention, but it is more desirable to have this module with its structured format, than none at all – relying on manual diaries and paper forms give much more opportunity for error.

Report writer

The report writer is essential for every system; without it, it is impossible to feed the organisation its life blood: information.

Of course, it has to be information that is relevant, and furthermore, it needs to be structured and accessible to those who need it most: boards and management.

This module should enable reporting on every field in your database, and automatically update its catalogue to add in any new fields. It should enable the results to be filtered by any given number of criteria such as dates, locations, ages, events and so on.

As far as the organisation is concerned, the effectiveness of your HRIS will be judged on its outputs, and that is pretty much down to your report suite. An operational suite could include the following:

Headcount:
> – Numbers of employees deployed through the organisation expressed as Full -Time Equivalents (FTEs) in order to ascertain the true resource required to run the enterprise.

Staff Turnover and Staff Stability:
> – Both reports are expressed through standard formulae to show the rates of attrition and retention within the organisation.

Salaries and Benefits:
> – A breakdown of the salary costs of the enterprise by department or cost centre

Absence by Department or Activity:
> – Demonstrating the impact and cost of a range of absence types in the units of an organisation

Objectives Met and Outstanding:

– Individually, within Department or enterprise-wide: monitoring the progress of an employee or activity in meeting their agreed objectives during the course of a prescribed passage of time.

Development Needs Met and Outstanding:
– Individually, within Department, or enterprise-wide: tracking agreed developmental actions for employees or groups of employees and when they are completed.

It would be well to remember that reports are only as good as the quality of the information within them. All too often, reporting from the HR department is found to be strewn with errors or outdated entries, and once the integrity of the data is questioned it is very difficult to get confidence restored in the output.

Departments will claim that they are under pressure, and this is understood, but reports are a highly visible product of HR and payroll functions and cannot be dealt with in a haphazard or sloppy fashion. Quality of data is paramount; self service (q.v.) solves part of that problem as responsibility for some elements of personal data passes to the employee or their manager.

For many years, the report writing features of most HRIS were particularly "user hostile" with very opaque terminology and not constructed with the typical audience in mind: day-to-day system users. Occasionally, these issues were compounded by poor vendor programming; failure to automatically update the report catalogue with new fields and in some cases the software was actually supplied with the fields not fully connected to the report writing catalogue.

Since those times, report writers have been considerably modified to make them more usable. The drive to do this has been, in part, in response to the fact that self service now permits levels of management to access the report generators, not just to use the standard suite of reports but to generate their own bespoke reports.

Self service

This module provides all employees with access to their personal records (address, contact, and emergency contact details) and their payroll records (bank account and payslips).

It is usual for employees to have the facility to change or modify certain fields such as Address, Bank Details or Emergency Contact, as well as generate requests for Holidays, Training or submit Sickness absence data.

Self service can also enable actions such as appraisal reporting online, connecting it to Objective Setting and training / developmental needs; these in turn can be approved and booked also through the module.

Access is usually either via an HR portal on an organisation's intranet or from a designated web link.

Layers of security within the application can permit managers to view records and requests relating to their staff or departments, as well as run or view reports specifically tailored for their own requirements.

Self service got off to a rather faltering start some years back; it was expensive to source and deploy, and the return on investment proposition was nebulous; organisations proclaiming that they had "empowered their employees" by allowing them to change their address and bank details clearly had failed to understand the implications of what was to follow.

Nowadays, self service is a standard feature of nearly all modern HR software.

Bear in mind that self service really only works well for organisations with populations able to access computers; the notions of "self-service booths" or expecting manual workers to log on at home have not been shown to be widely accepted.

Fortunately, technology has come to the rescue, and the majority of software vendors are developing "apps" for smart phones, so the problem of access for all may well fade away in time.

Talent management

Talent management is the current generic name given to the process of recruiting, managing, improving, evaluating and developing the employee base of an organisation and is, in essence, It is the end-to-end process of planning, recruiting, developing, managing, and compensating its employees.

Talent management software solutions aim to collect elements of what were hitherto disparate activities (Recruitment, Performance Appraisal and Development) and relate them back to organisational objectives.

With many vendors, talent management is an integrated module within the software suite, but there are also a number of stand-alone applications that can be harnessed to the main HR system. I am personally not a great fan of the "best of breed" concept, as interfaces need to be developed, and every time a version of one or the other changes, the interface needs to be updated, and all this can be very costly in the long run.

It is worth noting that someone who is really experienced in HR systems could actually bolt together their own version of talent management by combining features already present in the software and reporting out on them.

Training administration

Rather like recruitment administration, this module has a significant element of manual work. Approved candidates are logged for their specific training courses, the courses are booked and dates, candidates and costs can be viewed on the system or by reports.

Feedback is often captured after the event, and also kept in the module, although this usually relates to the course location and content, rather than any subsequent behavioural improvement.

Now let's look at a selection of features within the HR software.

• **Auto Number Generation**

Once set up (in system administration) unique employee numbers are generated as soon as a new employee is entered onto the application.

Existing sequences are loaded into the application providing that they can be accommodated by the HR software. It is good practice for employees to have only one number, irrespective of the number of posts or roles they may hold, particularly if there is a payroll software involvement.

• **Data Importer**

A data importer is a software feature that runs a routine to move data from one application to another. This can usually mean that data, e.g. in Excel format, is converted into another format (e.g. csv, comma separated values file) and then drawn into another application to populate it.

Most new or upgraded HRIS are populated by this method as it saves keying in all the data again. An application is populated by data held in several relational spreadsheets set out in a specific format.

This emphasises the need to ensure that all data is clean before migrating it to another application.

• Employee Relations

Employee Relations is the generic term for the part of the HR software that covers Discipline, Grievance and Appeal. The stages of these processes are tracked through the application, and will generate reminders where required. Not the least important of these reminders is the one that can be set up to purge warnings from the system in line with organisational policy.

• Organisation charts

These charts offer a graphical representation of the organisational structure, and are derived from the hierarchy on the database. Formerly, it was usual for this to be performed by third party software bolted into the (the best-known being Crystal, Impromptu and OrgPlus). Nowadays, most suppliers have their own charting software built into the application.

Modern organisations do not conform to the traditional pyramid structure, and are complicated by matrix reporting lines and multi-posts; there are occasions when the application has to be manually overridden on the chart itself to reflect a particularly complex arrangement.

• System Administration

The System Administration module is the part of the application where authorised persons are able to configure rules (such as Holiday and Occupational Sickness), add / delete new posts or modify existing ones such as amending the FTE, Departments and Divisions and add system users with their appropriate security access levels.

Additionally to this, the System Events (or Triggered Actions) and Work Flow functions can be formatted and set in motion from here, where available to the application; eventually this can be passed down to other users. The selection and appointment of system administrator/s will be an important decision to make further down the road.

• Triggered Actions

These are not only an invaluable "admin-killer" for HR, but they are very useful in helping busy managers to ensure that nothing falls down between the cracks.

Also known as system events, triggered events or automated events, these are featured in most HRIS. Responses are triggered by changes in specified data fields, and normally are embodied in email alerts to one or more relevant parties.

An example would be when a new employee is entered on the HR database prior to starting date, the configured triggered action would generate a series of emails to:

- **Advise security & switchboard of the arriving newcomer, name, position and department**
- Advise the IT department to create an ID and login;
- Advise the relevant departments to provide a car, mobile phone, laptop, where appropriate;
- Advise the training co-ordinator to enter the new starter on the next Induction programme.

And so on.

The effect of all this activity prior to commencement is to prepare the ground for a new hire, ensuring that they are fully equipped and functional from Day One; anyone who has experienced the frustration of not being able to access the organisation's computer system or not showing on the switchboard telephone list will appreciate how such basic administration makes all the difference to a new employee, and is key to the retention process.

A triggered action – or series of them – is set up in the System Admin part of the application. They constitute one of the big advantages of HR systems, as they streamline administration and help to suppress errors and oversights.

Typical support for managers will come with the following reminders:

- Probation periods
- Appraisals
- Unfulfilled Training Needs
- Service Entitlements
- Holiday conflicts
- Sickness Absence trends
- Company Property – laptops, mobile telephones, and security cards – issue on joining, return on leaving.

Did I say "admin-killer" for HR? Not only can you set up email alerts within your organisation, but you can generate messages to reach outside, for instance Starters and Leavers to the following providers:

- Life Assurance scheme
- Permanent Health Insurance scheme
- Medical Insurance
- Pension
- Company Vehicles

You need to remember that triggers cannot work for data already in the system: it will only react to changes made after the trigger was introduced.; for example if you build a trigger to alert you of probation periods expiring in the next month, it will only advise you of those that have been entered after the trigger.

- **Work flow**

One extremely important development that has accelerated since the advent of self service has been the enabling of work flow, the automation of whole or parts of processes where information, tasks or documents are streamed across the application. An example would be an employee returning from sickness completing an online form, which is then routed to their immediate reporting head for approval, upon which the form either heads for HR & payroll for the relevant processing, or is fed into the HR & payroll software automatically for action.

Work flow has made a big impact on the reduction of administration time and the suppression of errors and tasks that "fall between the cracks". However, it takes considerable thought and care to set up, and it is essential to map out the processes and test how logical and robust they really are; I still smile remembering the CEO who ended up coming back from leave with 78 holiday and sickness forms for authorisation in her inbox. Why? Because lower in the hierarchy, default approvers had not been written in correctly for absent managers, and tasks that could not be approved escalated upwards!

It is recommended that very basic administrative processes that currently exist are mapped as part of the new software application training; more complicated ones can be structured as user confidence grows. If you already have a system that has this feature but you're not using it, then set aside some budget and get your people trained properly in its use.

B. Payroll module and features

Payroll is normally delivered in the one module, although there are optional add-ons available such as applications for

- P11D (see Glossary)
- Expenses payments.
- Pension modules to handle auto-enrolment automatically.

Features for payroll will include facility for

- Online payslips (e-payslips)
- Grossing up salary (paying a required net amount and computing backwards to arrive at the gross figure)
- Capability to pay weekly, calendar monthly, four-weekly or other required interval.

Payroll software will come with the suite of annual and monthly statutory reports already configured

C. Time & Attendance module and features

Again, although time & attendance software comes in one module, there are a number of features contained within it.

Clock-in options

Many time & attendance products will offer a variety of sign-in options, including:

- Logging in to a computer, or via internet
- Biometric recognition (fingerprint, retinal scan)
- Swipe card
- Clock punch

For physical recording, readers need to be set up at entry points. In some software, these entries also constitute an entry system for access to premises. When you come to start compiling budgets for this type of software remember that the reader units are relatively costly, so you need to study carefully how many points you really need.

Record edit

Capability for supervisor or other authorised person to edit an attendance record. For example, if a person has not arrived for work and has rung in sick, the supervisor can edit the record from "no show" to "sick".

Shift creation

More complex than working patterns to be found in HR software are the shift configurations in time & attendance.

In addition to the setting of shifts assigned to each employee is the capacity to assign them to specific work activities, allowing job costing, the measurement of resources allocated to each of those activities, and the monitoring of them in real time.

A basic appreciation of the flow between the three main modules is shown in Fig.2. The information that flows between HR and the payroll and time & attendance modules is essentially static in nature: annual salary, job title or departmental change, starter or leaver. That which runs from time & attendance to payroll is mobile, overtime, absence, bonuses. Time & attendance can also feed back to HR to populate the absence module if required.

Now we are better armed with is background, we can now turn to some of the reasons why we need to get new HR software.

	MODULES	FEATURES
HR	Core database	Auto numbering
	Absence	Audit trail
	e-learning	Data importer
	e-recruitment	Employee relations
	Performance	Multi-currency
	Recruitment admin	Multi-language
	Report writer	Organisation charting
	Self service	System admin
	Talent management	Triggered actions
	Training admin	Work flow
PAYROLL	Main module	Online payslips
	Main module	P11D
	Main module	Expenses
	Main module	Grossed-up pay
	Pensions module	Auto-enrolment
TIME & ATTENDANCE	Main module	Clock-in options
	Main module	Record editing
	Main module	Shift creation
	Main module	Job costing and activity management

Fig.1: Chapter 2 summary grid

Data						
Starters, Leavers, Changes	▶	HR	▶	Payroll		
		HR	▶	Time & Attendance		
Attendance, Overtime				Time & Attendance	▶	Payroll
Attendance, Absence				Time & Attendance	▶	HR (Absence Module)

Fig. 2: Data flows between the HRIS

CHAPTER 3

PROJECT PRELIMINARIES

REASONS FOR SOURCING NEW SOFTWARE

Understanding the reasons why new software is required is crucial to understanding the process that follows, and informs the business proposition. In any organisation, there will be political dimensions as well as fiscal and operational issues.

Why do we need HRIS software? Here are some of the most commonly stated ones:

- No software currently
- Current software not fit for purpose – outgrown or inadequate
- Current software support being terminated
- Relationship with current vendor
- Need to economise on headcount and resources
- Changes in organisational technology
- New HRIS to replace disparate unconnected systems.

Let's look at each in turn to fully appreciate what is happening.

Although this sounds absurdly obvious, it is important to establish why you are looking for a new HRIS. Many times it has been seen that this aspect has not been fully thought through, and as a result, the project may be presented in a light that is not relevant to what you are trying to achieve.

Some of the more common reasons for organisations that **do** currently have an HRIS are:

-Software contracts traditionally included an annual fee for maintenance and upgrades, usually between 17.5-22.5% of the original software licence cost. As software has become considerably more economical to source, you could now be paying high maintenance for an outdated product.

-Is your current application giving up support of its product due to obsolescence or withdrawal? Vendors should give ample notice of this, and will generally point you in the direction of a more recent iteration of their offering.

-Is the software you have not doing the job it should for you? As organisational requirements become more sophisticated, software can easily become outpaced in its race to meet the case.

-Have you reached a poor stage of relations with your current vendor for whatever reason, and don't wish to continue with them?

-Has the size of the organisation varied dramatically so much so that either the current application is not scalable upwards, or headcount reduction means that it is now out of proportion to the number of employee records and operational requirements?

-Perhaps a new senior officer of the organisation has reviewed current capability and has decided that more advanced HRIS will deliver more benefits. It is not unknown for seniors to try to bring across the same systems as used in their previous employer, which would appear to be a comfort zone for them rather than a business need. It is important to remain objective: the previous employer may have had a completely different set of criteria.

For those currently **without** computerised systems, it is usually in response to up-scaling of the organisational size, compliance issues, or requests for more detailed management information, although the cost of maintaining manual systems nowadays will also figure uppermost in the business case.

Some of these above may be already familiar to you. In all cases I would urge you to review the position, maybe even with an HRIS expert and see what your options could be. It is possible that the software that you have could actually do the job for you with more focus on what you need and some collaboration with the vendor. After all, no vendor will willingly lose a customer!

The case for sourcing a new HRIS can also draw heavily on factors outside of the sponsoring department; HRIS are tools to assist service departments such as HR and payroll to contribute effectively to their organisation (the need for time & attendance also has its roots in operational and commercial needs). For this reason alone, it is a good time to go back to the internal / external "customers" and ensure that your thinking and expected departmental output is aligned with their requirements of you. In this way, you will strengthen support for your proposal when the time comes to pitch for the resources.

Whilst on the topic, one of the necessary evils may be to solicit at least tacit approval from internal political influencers, even though they themselves may not be directly impacted by a change. I have seen projects torpedoed because the sponsors failed to win political support. As I said: evil, but necessary.

A. WHO SHOULD BE INVOLVED: the project team

The composition of the project team will very much influence the success or failure of the project. Ensure that you choose the right people.

It's never too early to start to plan and build your project team, even before the selection process is fully under way. In fact, you will probably end up using different specialists at various stages of the entire project, with a permanent core of people at the heart of the project.

For every project, there should be a project sponsor, and our project is no exception

The sponsor should be of sufficient weight in the organisation to be able to defend their corner, and for an HRIS would most probably be the HR director where applicable. A sponsor for a new payroll system would most likely be the Finance director, and so on, depending to where the various functions report.

It is advisable to have a steering group to view the project from a top level, and this group must have authority to make radical decisions. The sponsor should be part of this, along with, perhaps, other seniors from Finance and IT, both of which departments are closely impacted by the project. Again, the composition of this group will depend very much on the organisational culture, but it is better to keep the number small, manageable, and decisive.

At this point I have a preference for forming a selection team, who will follow through the processes of articulating what is required, issuing a brief, oversee the tendering procedure, manage the demonstrations and ultimately influence the choice of software. This selection team should be headed by the appropriate person who will respond to the steering group throughout this phase.

Once the selection is made, the project becomes live, and that is when I recommend that the project manager is brought on board.

Reporting directly to the steering group, the project manager, who will communicate progress at agreed intervals, make recommendations and troubleshoot issues where necessary.

If there's one message to get across here it's **YOU MUST** get your own project manager; do **NOT** rely on the vendor to project manage on your behalf as they will ultimately fail to meet everyone's expectations, no matter how hard they work. They will always have difficulty balancing priorities that will occasionally be in conflict. You wouldn't expect a lawyer to act as both prosecutor and defender at the same time!

Importantly, having your own person will give more ownership, and that the introduction of your new HRIS isn't just something remote "happening" to your organisation

Let's get this in context: the project manager is unlikely to be able to combine the role with another day job.

The project manager must have experience in interpreting the vendor's plan, marshalling (and cajoling) resources, meeting deadlines and liaising with the vendor.

It's not a job for the amateur.

It's very tempting for, say, an HR manager to assume the role, but it is inadvisable unless they have the above-mentioned experience. Really – trust me on this one.

Ideally, you should use someone with the relevant experience from elsewhere within the organisation who can look at the picture dispassionately and impartially. Doing it this way, the experience stays in the organisation. Failing this, hire an external project manager; it won't be cheap, but having committed yourself to the solution you are not improving your chances of success by skimping on the essentials.

An option to reduce external costs can be to appoint a programme manager to oversee your internal project manager if the project manager's overall experience of this type of implementation is not comprehensive.

The programme manager brief will involve taking a broad view of the project, and review – probably on a weekly basis – with the project manager. In this way, the contractor expenditure is minimised, and the programme manager can provide a mentoring role.

Whoever lands the project manager position **MUST** have discretion to take decisions (within budget and other agreed limits) and have priority access to resources when required with causing unnecessary interruption to normal activities. It is essential that all affected departments are consulted during the planning of the project on all matters that affect their people and resources.

Working with the project manager will be any staff co-opted to work on the project, or departmental staff needed to give some time from their day-to-day work to assist on aspects of the project, usually on clarification or investigation of procedures or processes. This latter is important, and during the life of the project, maximum co-operation from all departments should be requested, to ensure that there is no delay caused by tardy information flow.

B. SCOPE

The first thing you will need to have is total clarity of the scope of your sourcing exercise.

Some of the earliest items on your checklist will appear straightforward, but in reality they generate a considerable amount of work to arrive at the correct answers.

- Do I need HR, payroll, time & attendance, or a permutation of these systems?
- What modules do I require: e.g. Absence, Recruitment admin, Employee Self Service, etc.?

It is then very tempting to start thinking in terms of features in these applications. This can lead to unrealistic wish lists, so think of how these things are actually going to be used. Remember the car analogy? We'll be looking at this aspect in the process mapping section.

Here are some basic considerations, apart from the operational and administrative ones, that you will need to address:
- How many locations will the software be serving?
- In what language/s will the application be used?
- Does everything have to be supplied by a single vendor?
- What is the preferred purchase basis? (rented, capital purchase)
- What is the preferred supply basis? (hosted by the vendor, managed or on own in-house servers?)

- What IT requirements are necessary to ensure compatibility with an incoming application? (of course, it can be an ideal moment to update some of the IT thinking as well!)
- How many users will I have – and who will be System Administrators?
- How much history do we bring forward?
- What happens to our old data if we need to refer to it?

At this juncture, you will also now be considering two further sets of options, one to do with delivery of your solution and the other to do with how you want to pay for it. There are many combinations to review, and although you are not in a position to know all the financial implications, it is the moment to appreciate which ones will work technically and culturally with the organisation's overall philosophy.

Delivery options:
- In house on own servers
- Hosted on vendor's servers
- Outsourced to a third party

Acquisition options:
- Purchase outright
- Lease or Rental (frequently based on an employee numbers per annum basis)
- There is, of course, Software as a service (SaaS):

Software as a Service is a fairly recent expression to describe the supply of software as a variable overhead rather than a fixed cost. In a sense, it is a new iteration of the "bureau" approach, but instead of a third party providing the processing as well as a software environment it is now supplied more flexibly.

Organisations can plug in and subscribe to services built on world-class infrastructure via the Internet. All they need is a basic computer with an internet browser and an internet connection. The trade-off for speedily being able to ramp up on an SaaS system can often be in the inflexibility of configuration that you need. As SaaS offers what is virtually a templated system, it may not be able to work for your organisation. Generally, the rule is that the simpler your processes and rules, the more likely that SaaS will be a live option for you.

SaaS also changes the traditional model of user licensing as on-demand licensing enables software to become a variable expense, rather than a fixed cost at the time of purchase. It also enables licensing only the amount of software needed versus traditional licenses per device.

Another upside to SaaS is that it can reduce the up-front expense of software purchases, and may lead eventually to a reduction of investment in server hardware as these costs and functions are shifted to the service provider.

At this stage, it's better to have an open mind on some of these issues until more clarity emerges about cost, ease of operation and organisational fit. However, these will need to be addressed over the course of the project, so it's as well to start drawing up your list at the earliest moment.

C. PROJECT STAGES

Finally, let's have a look at what we'll be letting ourselves in for. The key stages of identifying, rationalising, sourcing and implementing an HRIS are:

Stage	Topic
1	Scoping the requirement (present and future)
2	Building and presenting the business case
3	Vendor research
4	Vendor invitations to respond to requirements
5	Vendor demonstrations
6	Decision
7	Project activation
8	Project implementation
9	Live
10	Post-project

Fig 3: Project stages

We now move on to the all-important business case.

CHAPTER 4

"WHO OWNS THE SOFTWARE?"

Not long ago I postulated the 3 Basic Laws of HR software, to firmly identify where ownership and responsibility lie, as a means of reinforcing HR (and payroll's) right to determine their own requirements.

The **First Law** states that *"HR will take responsibility to ensure that their organisation has an HR system configurable to meet its process and information needs."*

Following on from the perception that HR analytics were invented ten minutes ago, are we saying that managements have been flying blind all these years? Well, yes, at least partially. I've seen the turmoil when an urgent request for employee information is handed down from above. Panic. The inaccurate and un-updated info in the system they have is exported into excel, and then hours of tweaking and manipulation, as unprocessed leavers, starters and changes are changed around. The report that eventually ends up with management is still strewn with inaccuracies at the end of it all.

From this arises the **Second Law:** *"HR will be responsible for the accuracy and timeliness of information held in the system, providing a single source of truth and real-time reporting."*

With the first two Laws functioning well, it's necessary to understand that HR's role is no longer to act as gatekeepers for the data. The data is organisational data, and needs to be available to all those authorised to use it.

Even now, a client HR director or manager will say to me "Great! Now we'll be able to give them those reports when they ask for them." Wrong. Those internal requests will disappear, because those needing reports will access them directly from the system whenever they need them.

Hence the **Third Law:** *"HR system information will be freely available and in required formats to all in the organisation authorised to have access to this information."*

Part of the blame for the all the disorder described above can be laid at the door of those same managements who insisted that Information Technology folk drove the selection process, on the basis that HR were not qualified to make these decisions. Well, looking over the years at the systems that IT selected, it seems they weren't too darned smart either, and their selection criteria completely discounted the user experience; sexy architecture, the ability to sit on their existing mouldering infrastructure, and compatibility with other outdated in-house systems were the keys.

Some of the problem also stemmed from HR being over-optimistic about what was to be delivered, and expecting vendors to configure the software with the minimum of input and time resource that they could make shift to provide. And, occasionally, to compound the problem, when the system didn't work as intended, they sourced a new one without correcting the previous approach.

That has now changed significantly, as the technology gets simpler and more intuitive, and the need for data has driven its own learning process. HR is now acutely aware of the needs of management, and is suggesting enhancements where these have not been specified.

My Three Laws aren't really anything revolutionary but I think it's well overdue that the responsibilities were formally stated and accepted. If HR has abdicated its role in ensuring that a functioning system is in place, if the data in the system is decidedly dodgy and if HR is still acting as a gatekeeper for management information, then it's time to change – and change now before change is imposed on HR.

CHAPTER 5

MAKING THE BUSINESS CASE

The business case is without any doubt the key part of the whole acquisition story. There's only really one chance to get it right, and if you don't it can lead either to low prioritisation or even postponement of the project. It is up to each organisation to set the bar for the required ROI in relation to the capital outlay.

Any vendor will confirm something that we and other consultants in the field have known for many years: this is a very "long tail" business; a major vendor recently told me the story of one prospect who finally signed on the dotted line FOUR YEARS after the initial contact!

A wide range of excuses are also given for delay or cancellation of supply contracts, consultancy arrangements: resources, restructures, a new HR or payroll Manager...it goes on. But what is the reason for this?

To me the answer looks very apparent: the sponsoring departments have failed to make a strong enough business case to make the sourcing of new or enhanced software *an absolute priority* for their organisations.

If the business case was strong, funding and resources would be available; Alan O'Neill, founder of **Totalamber Ltd** is renowned for his saying "decision is easy when value is clear". If value had been established in the formal business case, the decision to go ahead *with expedition* would have been a no-brainer.

The majority of business cases I get to see have already been presented by the time I get involved. In my mind, when meeting those concerned and reviewing the organisational requirements of these clients it's clear that they need new software, or possibly need to invest more in the applications that they have and the people who are working with them.

Why? In many cases, they are not making the most of available technology.

The use of admin-busting tools such as triggered alerts and workflow is very patchy, and there are various "work-arounds" outside of the systems due either to lack of knowledge or system inadequacy.

The business case must be predicated upon any or all of these basic factors:
- An identifiable return on investment
- Sourcing new software or (in some cases) investing in existing software will save money. Using newer technology means reduced IT resource required, in terms of people and hardware, e.g. servers
- The investment will bring about the suppression of errors
- Management will have access to better quality information, e.g. organisation charts, reports, and find it simpler and quicker to comply with statutory information requests
- New software saves time - literally
- New software reduces time-wasting administration, possibly leading to reduction in headcount, or re-deploying freed-up resource to other more important tasks, if that is possible
- Any other elements

Above all there must be a demonstrable and significant advantage over what is currently used. Let us examine in more detail the factors shown above.

1. Return on investment (ROI)

One of the questions your finance people will want answered is: what is the return on investment if you source a new system? For sure, there won't be any decision made based solely on ROI; that is only one way of looking at the proposal, but you need to have these figures available.

In order to compute the ROI on your HR & payroll System you first need to understand the concept and the metrics.

Broadly, ROI is expressed as a percentage over a given period of time. For an HRIS a sensible life span calculation would be 5 years, bearing in mind sector changes due to acquisition and technology change.

To arrive at a simple ROI, you must first fix the metrics, and then convert the outcomes into cash terms. This is applies to any form of comparative investment.

Basic metrics would be:

Net Benefits:
These are the Gross Benefits over the life of the application minus ongoing costs such as Interest.

Time Period
The defined life of the application.

Initial Costs
The total cost of the application; for calculation purposes, the initial consultancy is capitalised, along with the software and any additional hardware required.

Let's take an example:
Original software was purchased 7 years ago and cost £300,000. The current annual maintenance/upgrade charge is 20% of the original purchase price, and therefore is £60,000 p.a. For simplicity, we will waive the issue of internal interest charges and write-down, as well as any cancellation charges.

A new system is estimated to cost £200,000

The projected annual maintenance is 17.5% i.e. £35,000 per annum.

Existing system:

Original purchase price	Annual maintenance (p.a.) @ 20%	5 year cost
300,000	60,000	300,000

New system:

Purchase price	Annual maintenance (p.a.) @ 17.5%	5 year cost
200,000	35,000	175,000

Therefore annual net benefits are £60,000 - £35,000 = £25,000

Net benefit over 5 years is £125,000

The formula used in the above (simplified) illustration is:

ROI = Net Benefit divided by the investment required and multiplied by 100

Thus: ROI = 125,000 (5 year benefit) divided by £200,000 (investment cost) and multiplied by 100, giving a return on investment over a 5 year period of 62.5%

It is up to each organisation to set the bar for the required ROI in relation to the capital outlay.

2. Sourcing new software or (in some cases) investing in existing software will save money

We will need to do a lot of work, and research, into pulling all the elements together, starting with comparing current versus projected costs. We've already looked at one element, the annual maintenance and upgrade costs of the software, so let's take a look at the complete picture.

Rental or purchase of software

As discussed above, in the ROI calculation, there are savings to be achieved by switching to modern software, as costs of acquisition and upgrade have come down significantly over the past few years.

Hosting and IT overhead

If you are hosting your current software on servers based on your premises, then you need to calculate the costs of having those servers, the time spent by IT people who have to look after them, and any time that IT may use supporting HR in troubleshooting.

It is usual for IT people to have to know something about the HR system in order to service it, so their time spent on this should be added to the calculation.

Having your software vendor host the application is rather more expensive, but you need to weigh this against the costs shown above, plus:

Disaster recovery of data is the responsibility of the vendor;

Upgrades are performed at the vendor's end, therefore eliminating the need for any intervention by client's IT staff, and, incidentally, removing the risk of errors in upgrades.

Troubleshooting is more easily handled by the vendor.

Using newer technology means reduced IT resource required, in terms of people and hardware, e.g. servers.

Using a web browser-enabled system hosted by the vendor essentially reduces IT's role to ensuring basic housekeeping items such as:

- The internet "pipe" has the right speeds and bandwidth;
- The compatible browsers and versions are present;
- Compatible versions of Word, Excel and so on are enabled, etc.

Their involvement will have become rather more peripheral. This means that not only can savings be achieved, but that IT staff time is freed up for other projects. The time saved can be applied to our savings schedule.

I have mentioned the possibility of investing in current software being of benefit. It can happen, for whatever reason, a client will ignore an enhanced product upgrade or new version from their current supplier, or perhaps have failed to implement certain modules such as absence or self service.

Don't write off your software without first examining what it could still do for you.

3. The investment will bring about the suppression of errors

Most errors in data occur because there are manual interventions between paper forms and the systems themselves. Every time there is this intervention – or even others in the process – the chances of error increase. Automation eliminates this risk.

Additionally, modern systems will stop things "falling down the cracks" which happens with manual diaries and other written records.

4. Management will have access to better quality information, e.g. organisation charts, reports and find it simpler and quicker to comply with statutory information requests, and all in real time.

The deployment of self service will facilitate the quicker updating of information, which in turn leads to more current reporting.

I can say with a high degree of confidence that most of the absence reports currently available to management do not reflect the true picture for the simple fact that in most HR or payroll departments is a pile of unprocessed self-certification or other sickness and absence forms, awaiting the sporadic attentions of some poor junior tasked to punch them in.

5. New software saves time

There can be no doubt that the above statement is true. I've run tests in the past to try it out, and have seen for myself. The one that sticks most in my mind is when I ran comparable transactions across two different systems, one 10 years old, and the other a very new one. Older systems tend to use more keystrokes and screens. The transaction in point was to reduce an employee's hours down from 35 hours per week to 17.5. The old system needed 6 screens and several keystrokes; the newer on was 3 screens and fewer keystrokes. Transaction time for the old was close to 1 minute 30 seconds; the newer system took just over 50 seconds.

If you can save 40 seconds on every transaction, and then multiply that by the number that are processed every month and year, that's a significant amount of time saved, which can be translated into money terms.

6. New software reduces time-wasting administration, possibly leading to reduction in headcount, or re-deploying freed-up resource to other more important tasks, if that is possible

A key move forward has been the transfer of the administration of absence recording, (encompassing sickness, holidays, maternity / paternity / adoption leave and other categories such as jury service), from paper-based methods or spreadsheets to an online system that can supply reporting data in real time.

This capability has now spread to activities such as the processing of performance reviews and the driving of induction, training & development programmes as an outcome from those reviews.

Where data is poor and / or the software is not user friendly, organisation charts are frequently assigned to secretarial or administrative staffs and executed in MS Visio or Excel. This sisyphean task results in charts are prepared on a parochial, division by division basis and in differing formats, and so no overall view is available. Modern organisational charting will automatically reflect all current changes and adjust the chart view accordingly, which can then be accessed via self service.

Additionally, the paper chase of raising requisitions and obtaining authorisations is eased by workflow of documentation by electronic means.

Do some sums to calculate the time (and therefore cost) of the process of paper movement relating to these activities. These will largely disappear if your new system is set up correctly.

7. Other elements

Other elements to consider:

a) Additional intangible current costs:

Inability to produce accurate key data such as holiday & absence, headcount, training, exit interview and talent data

b) What is the overall effect of manually initiated systems that fail to manage, for example, with your current recruitment process, what negative effect are your manual systems having on the candidate experience during the following?

- Recruitment experience
- Smooth on boarding
- Transition through probation
- Progression through induction and development

These two above are only aspects of the current problem you may be experiencing, and they need to have a value attached to them.

For the former, you will need to talk to internal customers, management and the board to evaluate the extent of the problem and its cost; the latter can be assessed by talking to recent successful candidates, and those that were offered jobs and declined. It is time-consuming, but will help to reinforce you in your case for a better solution.

Over a period of some 10 years, the HRmeansbusiness Ltd consultancy has looked at the effect of changes in HR & payroll software on some of their clients.

This is largely by observation, talking to the clients and drawing some conclusions from these.

The figures are considered by us to be conservative, and are based on an organisation of 1000 employees, showing the time savings (expressed in FTE) achievable over a 5 year period by introducing the following features:

- Self Service   5.00
- Work Flow   1.25
- Report writer   1.25
- Triggered (automated) actions   2.00
- Organisation Charts   1.25

If your current system is more than 5 years old, then an additional saving of 1.00 FTE, BUT: if you currently have the features and are not using them, we discount the savings from above by 50%.*

Example 1

Our average company is proposing to acquire a new system that offers them additional benefits of self service and workflow.

New module and features	FTE gain
Self service	5.00
Work flow	1.25
Total gain over 5 years	**6.25**

They can add 6.25 FTE savings over 5 years to their business case. The conversion of FTE into cash terms will very much relate back to perhaps average salaries in the organisation.

Example 2

A similar company is changing its system, but in fact they had not been using Self Service or Organisation Charting in their previous software even though it was present. The software being replaced is 9 years old.

	FTE gain	FTE deduction
New software	+ 1.00	
Self service	+ 5.00	-2.50
Organisation charting	+ 1.25	-0.625
Sub total	+7.25	-3.125
Total gain over 5 years	+4.125	

(Derived from empirical studies by HRmeansbusiness Ltd over a 10 year period)
Copyright © HRmeansbusiness Ltd 2015

They can add 1 FTE to their savings for the age factor, but only 3.125 FTE for the two features as they benefit only by 50% (5.00+1.25 x 50%).

One question we are frequently asked about the above is from what areas of the business the FTE savings we show are actually to be made. These calculations are merely aimed at time saving related to the use of software features and not at individual departments, but by their very nature they are a benefit to the whole organisation.

Summary

Making the business case and getting it accepted is the cornerstone of your project, so it's worth remembering these guidelines:

- It has to be right first time: fall at this fence, and you may not even get a second chance at it.

- Everything in the proposal must be aligned with the organisational aims: If it's not helping your business and its aims, it is an irrelevance.

- It must be in scope with the size and resources of the organisation: don't buy an oversized or overpriced big name system on the "nobody got fired for buying IBM" principle. Make sure it is scalable both ways and as future-proofed as one can reasonably assume.

- Be specific in your requirements, and build all the assertions in your case on solid facts and figures. Any CFO / finance director will laser in on any airy-fairy assumptions e.g. (and I have seen this quite a few times): "Having a new absence management module will achieve a saving on absence of 20%". No it won't, it will be managers having access to the information that will make that saving - or not.

- The case must be compelling: we MUST do this or (list the downsides if we don't), and most importantly, it must be defined as a business priority. I've seen a good number of projects cancelled or put on hold because of higher prioritisation of other issues requiring the resources. The signature is not enough there must be a commitment to carry it through.

- Express time savings in terms of FTE: it's not a quantum leap for the people looking at your plan to start attaching a monetary value to those figures.

There is, regrettably, a political dimension to all this, so be very careful to get all onside, even those who would appear not to be directly affected but may have influence. Failure to consult with them at the very least could prove injurious in the medium term: this is where your project sponsor should be wheeled out and smooth the way for you.

When you have the system in and running, remember the promises you made about savings and efficiencies, otherwise all those good things in the business case will come back to haunt you!. I should mention here that any argument about freeing up HR's time for more strategic or "higher value" activities should be tempered by the fact that that it is not always possible to re-position people more suitably qualified for administration work into those more valuable roles. Some losses may arise over time, so it's as well to be prepared for this eventuality.

One last word of caution: do not forget to show in your calculations the cost of cancelling your current system early, if such is your situation. If you don't do this, not only will you appear to have been shoddy in your approach, you will antagonise the sponsors with unbudgeted cost. Study the contract carefully, and solicit advice if necessary.

If your contract is actually expiring somewhere around the time of the new system coming on stream, then your best option is to ask for an extension on a monthly – or at worst, three monthly renewable basis until you are able to make a final determination on the future of the existing contract. I haven't seen this refused yet, as, yes, vendors don't like losing a client, but it's a time to tread carefully!

CHAPTER 6

THE PROJECT INITIATION DOCUMENT (PID)

At this stage you will have a file with a pile of papers relating to this project. Many of these will form what is known in formal project circles as a Project Initiation Document (PID) which when complete will contain something very similar to this:

- The project aims
- Scope of the project; what will be – and not be – within the project
- The business case
- Those who will be affected by the project and are therefore crucial to its success
- What are the identifiable risks or threats to the project
- Overview of the limits of responsibility for all involved in the project
- Reporting lines within the project and to the outside
- Protocols for changing aspects of the project whilst in progress

These can be gathered together to be signed off by the sponsor and other appropriate parties to give assent not only to the proposed spend, but also the proposed methodology.

At times you may need to revisit this file for confirmation that the project is running in the intended direction.

CHAPTER 7

IMMEDIATE ACTIVITY - 1

Marshal Suvorov: "Train hard – fight easy". The work you do now will repay itself many times over later on.

Even as the new software project is taking shape, there are a number of important things that must be done in the interim; these things will save time as the selection and implementation stages loom, and money in terms of external consultancy costs.

We now enter the phase which, in previous times, was seriously overlooked, resulting in a knock-on effect of potentially catastrophic proportions.

In my workshops on selecting and implementing HR & payroll software, I have gone to great lengths to describe the actions that need to be taken before the project gets under way, in terms of data, hierarchies and rules.

The original thrust for this was to reduce vendor consultancy time, but it also pays dividends in terms of speeding up the implementation process.

It will no longer be appropriate for clients to blame the software or the vendor for shortfall or inefficiencies in performance that stem from their own imperfect structure, data or processes or even personnel. They will also have to take these projects seriously, and ensure that appropriate levels of resource and priorities are assigned to them. If in-house expertise is not available, then they need to bring in outside help to position them for their project.

The very mention of the new project stimulates a desire to run off and look at software, because that's the sexy thing to do, but right at this point it's the last thing we should be doing. We can now consider some of the key actions we should be taking as soon as the project has approval, and these fall into the following categories:

- Data quality and data cleansing;

- Documenting the current (and envisaged future) IT environment;
- Organisational rules (*Chapter Seven*)
- Review, mapping and documentation of current processes;
- The product specification

Data quality and data cleansing

In my consultant capacity a question I always ask is "how good is your data?" Replies will vary from "pretty good" to "not too good" but always accompanied with a metaphorical shuffling of feet. Let's face it, it's generally poor in quality, and this can happen for a number of reasons, principally:

- Inconsistency in posting protocols, e.g. addresses not all aligned in an agreed format
- Lack of control in system administration, e.g. no consistency in job titles or departments
- Incompleteness of records: many employees have data missing because it wasn't present during the original entry and not followed up OR some data categories missing altogether from the system, e.g. ethnicity
- Information is not current as no updates have been requested on a routine basis; for some categories there may be a backlog for entering, a common problem with absence. There may have been movements between posts and departments that were not recorded on the system at the time.

The quickest way to solve this is to request an information update from all of the staff, either by printing out what you already have, or by circulating a new blank form. I favour the latter approach, as it gives an opportunity to include data fields that you didn't originally use or have on your system.

Make sure that the person/s tasked with updating this information on to your current system are familiar enough with the data to be able to sense check it, and that the entry guidelines are clear. When the exercise has been completed, run a full report from the system and check it back to the individual sheets. Of course it's tedious, but it is extremely necessary, and that is understating it. If you ever want to instantly destroy faith in the new system, or even the department's ability to use it, then run off and circulate a report with incorrect data.

Documenting the current (and envisaged future) IT environment

It is important that any new software will accord with the environment and philosophy of your IT function, so, irrelevant of whether the software will sit on your own servers or not, start to gather together a profile of your current IT set up, together with details of any anticipated changes over the life of the software.

- Which operating system is used, e.g. Windows 10
- Which version of Internet Explorer or other standard browsers used
- Which version of Outlook
- Which version of MS Office
- What type of internet connection plus speeds and bandwidth
- Specification of servers if used

All of this information will be available from your IT department, and it is worth starting the discussion early. Once the search is well under way, some vendors may request additional information; ensure that if questions are routed directly to the IT department, there is a record of these requests and their responses so that there is no delay in the flow of information.

CHAPTER 8

IMMEDIATE ACTIVITY – 2

Organisational Rules

Rules for an HR system are all the factors that need to be configured into the system to ensure that it reflects company policies and procedures

There are two sets of rules: statutory and those set by the organisation (organisational).

Statutory rules are set by Government and standard across every organisation.

These will include:

- Statutory Sick Pay
- Statutory Maternity, Paternity and Adoption Pay
- Statutory Holiday Entitlements
- Minimum Wage parameters

Your software will have these already configured, and they are automatically updated when any changes occur.

Organisational rules are particular to that organisation and may affect Occupational provisions such as Sick Pay, Long Service Entitlements, Pay Grades and Organisational hierarchy.

These will include:

- Occupational Maternity, Paternity & Adoption Pay
- Occupational Sick Pay
- Holiday entitlements (plus any enhancements for e.g. service)
- (These three above will reflect any entitlements over the statutory minima)
- Overtime multiples (where the calculation is done inside the payroll module) or shift premiums.
- Work Locations

ORGANISATION

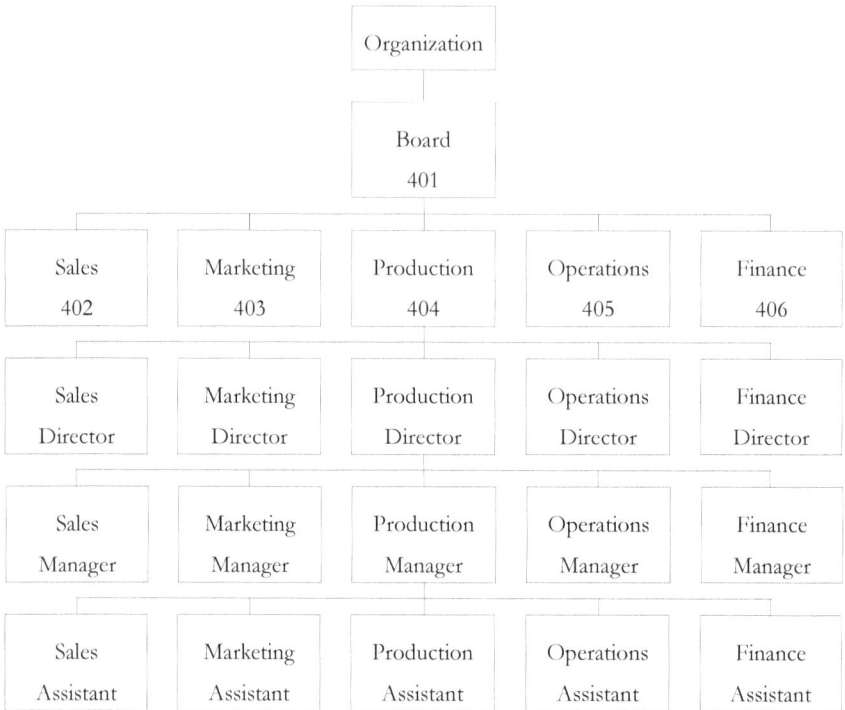

Fig. 4: Organisational Structure

- Organisational and Departmental structure
- Grade structures, entitlements and salary bands
- Post attributes such as budgeted FTE (full time equivalents), working hours and working patterns.
- Company property allocated to certain posts (e.g. laptops, mobile phones)
- Approval limits and protocols. These will be essential where any form of work flow is integral to the system. Approval limits (usually for salaries or bonuses) and action approvals (ability to recruit, perhaps within certain budgetary limits which are also held in the system) will all need to be tabulated so that they can be configured.
- Organisation-specific fields such as Fire Officers, First Aiders or Appointed Persons
- Visa or Work permit data

Rules are easier to compile and understand in graphic form, in the shape of matrices or tables. We shall now look at some of these tables and the type of information contained in them. These matrices are vital to the configuration process as we shall see later.

DEPARTMENTS & POSTS

	Location	Grade	FTE	Working days	Hours per week	Budget Salary £
Sales 402						
Sales Director 40201	A	2	1	M-F	37.5	50,000
Sales Manager 40202	A	3	1	M-F	37.5	35,000
Sales Assistant 40203	A	4	0.8	M-F	37.5	18,000

Fig 5: Posts and Conditions

ORGANISATIONAL STRUCTURE

In this very simplified diagram (*Fig. 4*), we see part of an organisational structure showing departments and the posts budgeted within those departments.

A reporting hierarchy can be seen; directors report upwards to the board, and posts beneath the directors report upwards through the levels.

Each department is also assigned a cost / profit centre code, and for universal ease of use, this code matrix should reflect the same codes as used by finance in the Chart of Accounts.

DEPARTMENTS AND POSTS WITHIN DEPARTMENTS

The grid in Fig.5 shows the Sales Department, and the conditions attaching to each post.

Note that each post carries an internal code, although this is purely optional.

The issue becomes clouded when an employee in fact holds two posts – both perhaps part-time – and reports to more than one manager. Some software applications cannot handle this without having two different accounts set up for the person, which is highly unsatisfactory, especially when it then impacts on the Payroll.

If you have what are known as multi-posts in your organisation, you will have to look very carefully at the vendor specification or ask the question directly. As a rule of thumb, most vendors who sell into the public sector will have this feature, by necessity.

Continuing on from the above, benefits attaching to each of the posts would look like Fig.6 below.

Note that each of these benefits carries either an actual or notional cost, reflected from the budget, which facilitates departmental costing and monitoring.

POSTS AND BENEFITS

	Grade	Ann. Car Allowance	Medical Insurance	Perm Health Insurance	Mobile Phone	Laptop
Sales						
Sales Director	2	Y 3,000	Y 750	Y 200	Y 200	Y 200
Sales Manager	3	N 0	N 0	N 0	Y 200	Y 200
Sales Assistant	4	N 0	N 0	N 0	N 0	N 0

Fig.6: Posts and Benefits

GRADE-RELATED CONDITIONS AND BENEFITS

This matrix shows all organisational grade-related conditions and benefits, from which the above diagrams were derived:

Grade	FTE	Working days	Hours per week	Budget salary	Car Allow.	Medical Inse.	Perm Health Ins.	Mobile phone	Laptop
					Y	Y	Y	Y	Y
2	1	M-F	37.5	50,000	£3,000	£750	200	200	200
					N	N	N	Y	Y
3	1	M-F	37.5	35,000	0	0	0	200	200
					N	N	N	N	N
4	0.8	M-F	30	18,000	0	0	0	0	0

Fig.7: Grade-related Post conditions

The beauty of creating a post structure that is then populated with incumbents is that it is then possible to report on exceptions or deviations from the budget, both for headcount and cost reporting purposes, as illustrated in Fig.8

If standard organisational hours are 35 per week, and the post in question, e.g. payroll manager, is a 35 hours per week job, then it will be considered to be 1 FTE (Full-Time Equivalent). If the post was only 30 hours per week, then it would be expressed on a headcount report as 0.85 FTE.

An employee working half time (17.50 hours p.w) in a job that has a 1 FTE budget will be shown as actual headcount of 0.50 FTE and therefore a saving of 0.50 FTE on that post.

HEADCOUNT & SALARIES

				FTSE	Hours per week	Budget Salary
Department Code		Sales 402				
Post		Sales Director	Budget	1	37.5	50,000
Postholder	A Smith	40201	Actual	1	37.5	48,500
Post		Sales Manager	Budget	1	37.5	35,000
Postholder	B Jones	40202	Actual	1	37.5	35,000
Post		Sales Assistant	Budget	0.8	30	18,000

Postholder	C White	40203	Actual	0.8	30	17,500
Post		Sales Assistant	Budget	0.8	30	18,000
Postholder	Vacant	40203	Actual	0	0	0

Budget Salaries:	120,000
Actual Salaries:	101,000
Variance:	20,000
Budget FTE:	3.6
Actual FTE:	2.8
Variance:	0.8

Fig.8: Departmental Budget- to-Actuals

SECURITY ACCESS MATRIX

Access policies differ from organisation to organisation, but one rule should be constant: employees must not be able to change their own records (except allowed fields) in Self Service environments although they should be able to see them (Read Only) and have them included in reporting.

Access can also be selective; for instance, you may wish to allow the Training department to see employee records relating to Job and Training History, without having access to personal and salary data, in-house Recruiters to see Job detail only, and senior management certain elements such as post history.

With Time & Attendance, the most common security set-up is to allow Shift Supervisors to edit their own shift workers' absence records. Non-attendance is edited in arrears when the cause for absence is known, and can then be shown as Unpaid, Sickness, Compassionate or made up later on the shift, etc.

Access issues will also arise in Time & Attendance, where the system is used for Access Control to a building or parts of a building as well as a Time Recording device.

Where your entire workforce has Self Service access, you will need to organise security levels for all. This will involve setting parameters for the fields that can be changed by all employees (address, bank details, absence and holidays), their managers and supervisors (approvals and training recommendations) and senior management (e.g. headcount, budgets and corporate communications).

Every post will need to have its own security access level. To avoid having to individually assess and code many hundreds of posts, the easiest way is to relate access back to grades. Here is shown an extremely curtailed view of a matrix that will need to be compiled for the configuration process.

Departments such as Human Resources or Payroll will almost certainly need to have access across the organisation and probably senior management too.

Access criteria will be along the lines of:

View: all departmental records for grade and below (e.g. Sales Manager can view his/her records and those of subordinates only)

Action: Can change post related fields of subordinates e.g. hours, salary, grade but not own fields

Action: can change own personal fields e.g. address, marital status, bank details, phone number

Additionally, nearly all software has an audit trial function that can either be stored electronically or printed out at prescribed intervals. This feature will supply details of date, transaction and who effected it.

SECURITY ACCESS			
GRADE	Access	Actions (Post related fields)	Actions (Personal fields)
1	All parts of database	Change all post related fields except e.g. salary	Change own personal details
2	Department only	Change for subordinates but not own record.	Change own personal details
3	Own record and below	Change for subordinates but not own record.	Change own personal details
4	Own record only	No	Change own personal details

Fig.9: Security Access Matrix

Work and Shift Patterns

Although shift working was traditionally associated with manufacturing, many service organisations also use them to ensure continuity of response.

A basic office working pattern could be: 5 days per week (Monday – Friday)

7 hours per day, 35 hours per week. On systems that capture time records, you may wish to specify hours, such as 0900 – 1700.

Many organisations will have differing working or shift patterns for their employees, and can range from weekly through to rotations that repeat every 12 weeks or more. Check that you have every available current shift pattern defined, and then add them to your rules folder.

You can then tie each employee to a particular work pattern.

Some workers are defined as "floaters" as they have no fixed pattern, but you can establish a no-shift category, and the shift supervisors can manually add them to shifts as required.

If you are opting for a time & attendance module, you will find most actually make setting up and editing shifts very easy indeed. A further refinement on some applications is analysis of specific work activities within shifts.

Sourcing a new time & attendance system is the right time to re-evaluate your clock-in points. The clocks are a significant investment for each unit, and so you really don't want too many of them. Study the dynamics of your operation as well; are your clocking points too far away from the actual work stations? Will there be bottlenecks at certain times.

There are a number of ways that employee clocking in can be done.

Best-known of these are traditional punch cards, where the card is passed through a clocking device which validates the entry or departure times; they have largely been replaced by swipe cards which slide through a reader to collect the information or proximity cards which are contactless.

For office-based or the increasing number of remote workers, there is the "web punch" or "PC punch" which can be operated either through one PC or decentralised to give each user a log in.

There will be more detail on this in Chapter 16".

Assembling all the rules is undoubtedly a major task, and I cannot emphasise enough the importance of doing it as early as possible. Why? Because when the project manager of your chosen vendor arrives to configure the system, you need to have this ready. These experts can be costing you nearly four figures a day - or more! -and it is wasteful for staff to run around trying to source this information while the meter is running. And, in all the haste, things will be overlooked.

CHAPTER 9

IMMEDIATE ACTIVITY - 3

Review, mapping and documentation of current processes

Setting out on your HRIS project is the ideal moment to revisit your key processes, and map them. This exercise will:

a) Inform you of any modifications to be made

b) Assist you in making comparisons between software vendors

c) Enable you to build scenarios for demonstrations

d) Give your selected software's consultant key information for configuration

The main transactional processes that we will probably need to consider are:

- Recruitment initiation and fulfilment.

This can encompass the whole run between a vacancy being identified and approved, recruitment through own module sitting on your website or via third parties, interview planning, offers and acceptance.

- Starters

Following on from the above, the stages from acceptance to on boarding a new recruit, including advising the organisation of their arrival on a certain date, which department, their entry on an induction programme, probationary review, and so on.

- Performance management process

How performance management is initiated at set intervals, by what deadlines the review must be completed, how performance is evaluated and rewarded if appropriate. Any developmental needs will be addressed in the following section.

- Learning & Development process

Leading on from performance review, how needs are identified, approved and delivered within a specified period, and reflected in the records.

- Transactional changes

Administrative actions for salary / position /department/reporting line, relocation, etc.

- Absence processes

How sickness is reported and recorded, holiday bookings and other absence types such as maternity/paternity/adoption, jury service, compassionate leave and other types.

- Employee Relations

All processes relating to the disciplinary, grievance and appeal procedures that should reflect that which is set down in the employee conditions or handbook. Many of these have prescribed response times wich must be adhered to.

- Leavers

How a leaver is processed from date of advice of termination until final day, and beyond in some cases, to include exit interview procedure as well.

These are suggestions; it may be more convenient for some organisations to bolt process stages together, or separate some to avoid them becoming too cumbersome for mapping.

I have found the ideal way to approach process mapping is to set up workshops with all personnel who are involved at any stage in the process itself and facilitated by a nominated person (usually me!) who will ultimately capture and record the revised process flow.

First I like to have the existing process set down, by annotating pieces of sticky paper with the various stages as described by workshop participants, and then laying them out end-to-end in the correct current sequence.

Once this has been established, it is then the task of the group to look at each stage objectively with a view to deciding if it can be improved by adding or subtracting actions or responsibilities.

A great example of process improvement was in one client session, where we found that five signatures were required to recruit a replacement employee: the hiring manager, their divisional head, the head of HR, the finance director and the managing director.

This incredible paper chase led to long delays in recruitment while the requisitions lay in in-trays awaiting attention or decision, and clearly this was detrimental to the business. This was overcome by approaching the finance director with the proposal that:

- Headcount was already agreed in the annual budget, together with a salary cap

- The hiring manager could be trusted to make the decision that a replacement was necessary.

- A finance operative could verify and approve that the proposed hire was within budgetary guidelines

- Two signatures (hiring manager and finance operative) were all that were needed to put a recruitment campaign under way, thereby saving some weeks of inaction.

Here are some suggested steps in this part of the on-boarding process. We shall see later on exactly how much impact a well-set up HR system can have on this same sequence of events, but it is clear that managing all these stages manually leaves a lot of scope for omission or untimeliness.

Stage	Action	Responsibility	Date req'd
	Letter of acceptance received, new employee starts in 4 weeks		

Stage	Action	Responsibility	Date req'd
1	Letter of acknowledgement together with: • Staff Handbook • 1A- Starter form for completion and return • Reminder for P45 • Reporting details on day 1 • 1B-Car or Car Allowance options (if applicable) • 1C-Life Assurance beneficiary form) • 1D-Medical Insurance form (if applicable) • 1E-Pensions information and joiner forms • 1F-Salary Continuation (Permanent Health) Insurance forms (if applicable) • Amount of pro rata holiday entitlement (after probation) for remainder of current holiday year.	HR	Immediate response
2	Receipt of completed forms		
3.	Enter starter details (from1A) on to system	HR & payroll	Immediate
	1B: If allowance enter on payroll	Payroll	
	1B: If car, contact supplier	Facilities via HR	
	1C: Completed form to insurer; copy to file	HR/payroll	
	1D:Completed form to insurer; copy to file	HR	
	1E:Completed form to pensions provider; copy and expression of wish to file	HR/Payroll: process deduction	
	1F: Completed form to insurer; copy to file	HR	
4	Advise Facilities for desk, telephone (and number) and equipment such as mobile phone, etc.	HR	Ready for day 1
5	Advise Security for entry pass	HR	Ready for day 1

Stage	Action	Responsibility	Date req'd
6	Advise Switchboard for inclusion on list	HR	Ready for day 11
7	Advise IT so that computer / laptop are available and access to all relevant systems is in place	HR	Ready for day 1
8	Advise Training & Development so that new starter can be added to in-duction	HR	Earliest in-duction date
9	Department Head to be advised of probation period completion date	HR	Immediate

Fig.10: Sample starter process

These current HR/payroll/time & attendance processes need to be evaluated in terms of their effectiveness, efficiency and resources needed to keep them running. Only in this way will you fully realise the benefits of the incoming new technology, and get smarter processes into the bargain; replicating out-moded processes on new software is just a waste of money and resources.

If you are short of in-house expertise and resources permit, use a reputable external person to check through those processes; their view will be objective, and will highlight weak areas that were never questioned due to their lon-gevity and having been "invented here". Contrary to a large body of opinion, these types of processes are broadly generic and not at all "unique".

Do not fall into the common trap of assuming that employee self service and work flow will solve all your problems at a stroke. It needs careful setting up, and most importantly, it needs considerable cultural management.

Once the process review is completed – and it should not be an over- lengthy exercise – you will then be armed with the prototype for your list of practical application features.

CHAPTER 10

THE PRODUCT SPECIFICATION

All the preliminary work we have invested so far will have informed us of exactly what it is we need. It's time to articulate these requirements into a recognisable format.

Having gone through the previous stages in a systematic way we now need to – metaphorically - commit to paper the specification of our required system.

As an example, using the lists of functions and features from the earlier chapter, we can state that we need an HR & Payroll system that:

Is integrated and has:

- Absence
- Automated triggers
- e-recruitment
- Organisation charts
- Payroll
- Performance management
- Report writer
- Self service
- Training administration
- Work flow

(The database function is a given).

This is the raw list. We now need to qualify what needs to be done by each of these requirements, so let's look at some examples, starting with module capabilities.

Absence

Must:

-be configurable for several types of absence

-show Bradford Factor scores

-show attendance charts in real time for company, departments and individuals

Should:

-facilitate computations for holiday entitlements remaining, maternity and paternity leave.

Automated Triggers

Must:

-enable emails both internal and external to the organisation

-populate template emails

-have the capability to deliver messages well in advance of events

-enable documents to be attached to the template emails

e-recruitment

Must:

-be compatible with the organisation's website in order to provide a recruitment portal there

-enable job vacancy posting, together with hiring manager data.

-should enable both standard templates and original c.v. to be transmitted, according to recruitment.

-client delivery – enable the sifting and response to candidates speedily and professionally

-contact delivery – enable the management and scheduling of interviews and follow up.

-should enable the integration of successful candidate files into the HR & payroll system.

<u>Should:</u>

-allow for qualifying questions to filter out unsuitable candidates before submission

Organisation charts:

<u>Must:</u>

-automatically reflect in graphic form the organisational hierarchies

-offer multiple options for labelling positions inside the charts

<u>Should:</u>

-export to Word or other medium

-have an option for organisational modelling.

Payroll:

<u>Must:</u>

-have ability for n number of pay and deduction fields

-enable e-payslips if required

-be able to pay weekly, monthly, or calendar basis

-be able to calculate reducing and accumulating balances

-have the ability to review payslips before committing

-provide a suite of reports, both statutory and configurable

<u>Should:</u>

-be HMRC or other government-approved

Performance management

<u>Must:</u>

-have capability to record set targets and timelines, and measure actual achievements against them

-allow for developmental needs to be identified and held open until closed by corresponding entry from training record to confirm the need has been met.

Report writer:

<u>Must:</u>

-automatically update additional fields to the report writer catalogue

-be able to filter between two dates or on any combination of present fields

-incorporate graphic representations

-be able to export to Excel

-Standard report formats attached, plus any future required reports currently not available

Self service:

<u>Must:</u>

-be accessible by application (App) or web link from any location

-Self service gateway should be accessible via gateway on company website, intranet, etc.

-Self service functionality must be in accordance with individual security settings

-enable access for personal data, absence, training and performance management in line with security settings

Training administration

<u>Must:</u>

-capture dates, employees, location, provider and costs of all training and development

-be able to cross reference to the performance management module when a training need there has been fulfilled.

Work flow

<u>Must:</u>

-have a logical assembly method with "wizard" style assistance

-enable documents to be moved around within the self service module according to set up

-recognise electronic approvals

Other

Audit

-there must be an accessible audit trail for every transaction, with date, time, ID and action taken.

Data export

-there must be capability to export data in files with either .csv or excel formats

Data Importer

-there should be capability for importing bulk data into the system

Deployment

-the system should be hosted by the vendor and accessible via a web browser, app, or other agreed method.

Document attach

-all records in the system should have a document attach capability for formats of MS office, 'jpg, etc.

Equal Opportunities Monitoring

-the system must capture all data relating to statutory EO requirements, and configurable for any other data specifically needed by the organisation

Security

-the system must only be accessible to those who are authorised, and to the levels of security to which they are configured.

-additions to or removals from the security register must take immediate effect.

Single sign on

-the system must be accessible via our existing single sign on routines.

Single Sign On (SSO) means that when a user logs in to one application they are automatically into other designated programmes as well; e.g. an accounts department employee signing into the self service system can also be entered simultaneously into the accounting software and their email account, meaning, of course that there is no bewildering array of Id and passwords for each piece of software.

System administration

-Only designated system administrators can set up or eliminate organisational units, posts, and other structural elements as laid down in the agreement.

The above list is not exhaustive, of course, but it is fairly typical, and serves to show the methodology and what its outcome should look like.

Notice we use "**Must**" and "**Should**" to emphasise the desirability of each item. "Must" is pretty much a deal-breaker, whereas "Should" is something that we would really like, but could possibly live without if all other aspects of the software met our requirements

You will also now see how valuable our process maps are; we can append these to any of the above sections to illustrate the level of configuration needed in order to meet our requirements, and from all of this emerges our specification document.

CHAPTER 11

FINDING VENDORS

To begin the search for a supplier, we need to know where to look to find them; it's important that we leave no avenue unexplored in to have the best possible choice available to us.

The next step now is to start looking for vendors to whom we can communicate our proposals. Let's look at the most likely routes by which this can be achieved.

- Desk research via internet

This is a route that seems the most obvious, but unfortunately it's not always the most useful. Try "HR & payroll software" in your preferred search engine. First you have to bypass the paid advertising, and when you've done that, the results are not always immediately relevant perhaps due to their geographical base, or some may not directly relate to just HR & payroll software.

- Ads in industry journals

This is a rich source for desk research, and there are some very handy software vendor directories incorporated in *People Management*, *Personnel Today* and the *Global Payroll Magazine*. Following the links that you find there, you can then visit the various websites gathering information.

- Specialised websites

There is a growing number of websites now dedicated to helping practitioners select HRIS, and here I must declare an interest.

In 2008 I was playing around with a series of algorithms to assist me in my consultancy work on selection. My problem was that I was at that time tracking over 100 systems associated with HR, payroll, time & attendance, recruitment and many others, and that it was time-consuming collating client requirements and comparing them with a very bulky spreadsheet.

After some searching around, I was able to source a good algorithm from a United States website (CompareHRIS), and then went one further by launching HRcomparison in mid-2009. HRcomparison shared a considerable amount of DNA with CompareHRIS to start with, but went on to develop its own particular style.

At that time, it was the only comparison website in the UK dedicated solely to HR & payroll software.

The inventory of questions inside this website were the culmination of years of consultancy Q & A, and designed to get an enquirer down to a long or short list as fast as possible.

HRcomparison itself is now being managed by the Global Payroll Association, who are developing it even further.

This type of website for HRIS is far more common in the United States. In the UK, the majority of sites are less detailed, focusing on modules, number of employees and budget. As we have seen already, the presence of a module does not guarantee that it can be configured to a particular client's needs. Budget also is a pretty loose measure; although software itself comes at a pretty stable price that can be quoted, the unknowns can drive this up in the form of project costs or unpreparedness on the part of the client.

All of these sites are free to use for the prospective buyer; vendors either pay to appear on the site, or pay per lead, so be prepared to give up your business details if you want to access results.

Whilst we are on the subject of comparing software, people often ask me why there is no "Good Consumer Guide" for HR & payroll software. Some reasons for this are:

- Anyone who bought the wrong system or failed to specify implementation correctly is going to give a bad rating: it's human nature. The same applies where the vendor was overly optimistic about the ability of their product to meet the client's needs.

- It is essential that the ratings that are being given apply to the same piece of software, the same version and pretty much the same configuration, otherwise there is no consistency, and products evolve, usually for the better. How could one compare, say a 2005 3 series BMW with its 2016 iteration?

- HR software is personal to the using organisation. It is configured differently, unlike, say a car that has a relatively limited range of options. The experience of one reviewer will differ substantially from that of another.

In HRcomparison, we did consider the issue, and concluded that results would not truly represent an accurate guide for the practitioner, and it remains my view, at least for the time being.

- Software shows

These shows very often afford you your first experience of the available software up close, and it can result in a rush of blood to the head! In the section on Product Demonstrations I shall be dealing in detail with how you should prepare for a software show so that what you do on the day gives maximum return for your time.

For many years the main shows were the *CIPD HR Software Show* (in June), *CIPD Conference & Exhibition* (November) and Softworld *(February and October)*. The latter now no longer take place as the company appears to have withdrawn from that market, and other similar exhibition attempts have failed to take root. Both the *CIPP* and *The Global Payroll Association* have a limited number of stands at their annual conferences. All of this means that your opportunities for open perusal are not as frequent as one would wish.

I anticipate a swift rise in the online exhibition phenomenon; not only do they eliminate travel and accommodation costs, but they are live 24 hours a day for the specified dates, with live contact during actual working hours. They also enable unhurried browsing in a rather more hospitable location than most exhibition halls which seem to share a capacity for fairly inaccessible locations, overheated halls and exorbitant catering prices.

- Contract a specialist

Another interest to declare here too: I am an HRIS selection specialist, but of course I am not the only one!

A specialist can save you weeks of– sometimes unfocused - research by re-viewing your brief (or helping you compile one if yours is not fully-formed) and pointing you in the right direction, not only as to what software vendors you should be including on your list, but also what to watch out for and what to avoid.

Considering the overall value of your project, it can represent a good invest-ment. A specialist will charge a daily fee plus reasonable expenses such as travelling and accommodation where appropriate.

The final thing that we need to do in our researches is to look at the cur-rent vendor contract (if we have one), because we certainly don't want any unbudgeted surprises. Check how long it has to run, and measure that time against your estimated go-live date.

If it is going expire before then, then get into conversations at an early stage about renewing on a one- or three-month rolling period, while you examine your options. This is by no means "goodbye", and is a reasonable step for any client as they approach the end of a contract.

If it is going to expire after the go-live date, then you need to look at the notice period to be given and the terms of any penalty. Dependent on the overall circumstances, it may be possible to negotiate, but jilted vendors don't always want to be kind, unless there is a well-documented history of poor support.

Whatever the penalty, if you have established the project as a business prior-ity, there should be no problem.

CHAPTER 12

TENDERING

Some of you will be obliged to pass through a pre-ordained tendering process; if you don't have your own process, consider devising one that will provide objectivity in your assessment of vendor offers.

Given that our researches have thrown up a considerable long list, we now come to the point where we need to talk about tendering and the tendering process.

Tendering is one method of trying to ensure that an organisation is going to find the best supplier and product to meet their requirements at the best value price. It also provides an opportunity for a current relationship to be assessed at arm's length. The underlying intention is that all potential providers can be allowed a level playing field in which to pitch.

All qualifying vendors will be equipped with the same documentation, required to answer the same set of questions, and allowed the same amount of time to demonstrate their wares.

This activity also has the notional benefits of ensuring compliance where regulation of such activity exists, e.g. in public organisations or corporations bound by internal or external legislation, and providing a trail that will stand up to audit if the selection or selection process is challenged.

If it all sounds perfect, unfortunately, in practice, it isn't.

Many organisations that are obliged to tender can be very risk averse and this can present the possibility of vendors being discounted for what are *prima facie* very strange reasons. I have seen suppliers not make the cut because their balance sheet was not considered robust, or because their payroll software was not HMRC approved (the latter is by no means a "must have).

Additionally, in their zeal to cram in every conceivable question, these specification documents can run to over 150 pages and I have seen some that exceed 200. The point is, only those players who are equipped to deal with these are going to be able to respond. A lean and effective vendor may not have the resources to spare on an exercise where, in fact, they may only be making up the numbers. In fact, many don't even bother with them, and that hardly stimulates a process of change in the market place.

To exacerbate things, some of those questions I have seen in the past include:

"The software must do what it says it can do" and "the software must enable the transformation of the Human Resources department into a change agent for the whole organisation". Yes, totally unreasonable, and yet I have seen these continually in my career, along with my personal favourite, "push-button reporting".

It would appear obvious, if only the larger vendors are more likely to respond, your room to manoeuvre is very limited, and so the idea of a level playing field disappears very quickly.

In public sector institutions tendering is compulsory if value of the contract will potentially exceed current EU guidelines, and large corporations also use tendering for prospective major contracts, developed to suit their own particular procurement rules.

In reality, most small to medium enterprises do not have a formal tendering procedure, and below I outline how they can produce their own working document.

When dealing with tendering, It should be noted that there are a number of different titles describing the same thing, and sometimes a confusing array of acronyms. I have tried to simplify this for the reader where possible.

Request for Information (RfI)

A written invitation or Request for Information (RfI) is sent to potential suppliers of HR & payroll software, time & attendance software or other HRIS, advising them about the information that will be required. Once a tender document is issued, the tender process can be considered to have begun.

An RFI can also be known as a pre-qualification questionnaire (PQQ). Typical information required would be financial statements, health & safety policies, equality policies and commentary on the resources available to service the prospective client, together with general and relevant experience related to the particular client request.

An RfI will follow a standard format, to enable easy comparison and assist the process of selecting a list of vendors who will then be invited to tender by means of a request for proposal (RFP), invitation to tender (ITT), request for tender (RFT) or request for quotation (RFQ).

Request for Proposal (RfP)

Also known as: invitation to tender (ITT), request for tender (RfT) or request for quotation (RfQ).

The RfP will include specifications of the item, project or service for which a proposal is requested. The more detailed the specifications, the better the chances that the proposal provided will be accurate. There will also be information about the manner of responding, to whom and by when.

Responses are analysed, scored according to criteria (these can be weighted) and a long or shortlist drawn up for product demonstrations.

Building your own tendering process for HR & payroll software

As I mentioned earlier, many small to medium businesses do not have a formal tendering process, and even if they do, it may only be applicable for the supply of certain specific goods or services.

Here follows an easy-to-follow format for anyone to compile their own tender process in the search for the right software. To do this, I have in effect merged the RfP and RfQ elements together to speed up the process. I have given sample statements that can be modified to suit individual cases.

Where a response is required, please indicate clearly. If a certain attribute is a "must have" please also highlight this fact, and clarify if the absence of said item will render an immediate rejection.

Stages:

1. **Introduction – who are we, what is our business, location, size and workforce.**

"The XYZ company manufactures widgets for both export and home markets.

There are a total of 670 employees distributed across 3 locations in the UK. HR & payroll functions are based in the head office.

215 employees are paid monthly and the rest are weekly paid.

Just over 500 employees are working shifts.

The company expects to expand its employee numbers up to by double over the next 5 years

2.   Scope of project – the scale of what we are proposing, e.g.

"The XYZ company is looking for vendors of HR & payroll software to tender for the provision of a system to be operational by 1st June 2017.

The new system will replace the current software which will no longer be supported at that date / which does not have the required functionality for our current / future requirements

XYZ intends to replace the current HR & payroll system with integrated software that includes modern functionality to eradicate unnecessary administration and improve the flow of information to assist the business both strategically and operationally.

It is intended that this replacement will be effected using as much current technical infrastructure as is possible without any adverse impact on performance.

The current time recording system is not within the scope of this project but some interface will be required from the new system to populate it.

3.   The organisation's current Technical environment e.g.

- Servers – specification

- Client/s - (is a piece of computer hardware or software that accesses a service made available by a server. The server is often (but not always) on another computer system, in which case the client accesses the service by way of a network. The term applies to programs or devices that are part of a client–server model)

- Internet

- Bandwidth

- Web browser and which versions? E.g. Internet Explorer 11, Google Chrome.

- which versions of Microsoft Office (e.g. 2010, 2013)

- which email client you use (MS Outlook, Windows LiveMail, IBM LotusNotes, Apple Mail)

I would advise that you ask your IT department to collaborate on compiling this and any other information they feel relevant, such as any planned changes in the overall environment.

4. **Current Business Systems –what other software you have in place e.g.**

- General ledger, debtors and creditors system is provided by vendor X (v.6)

- The current HR & payroll system is 123 for Windows as supplied by vendor Y on a 32 bit platform. This system has been in operation since 2008

- A stand-alone time recording application, 456 (by vendor Z) is used, but not currently connected to the main HR & payroll system.

5. **Functionality and Features required (drawn from our earlier findings) e.g.**

A Human Resources application that will accommodate the current numbers of employees, is scalable, and comprises the necessary elements to maintain secure data, reduce administration and provide quality reporting for operational purposes.

Fields must be configurable and there must be the ability to add fields which automatically populate the Reporting catalogue.

We will wish to import some Career History from the current application.

Capability of allowing varying levels of security access according to user.

The specified modules are:

- Core Employee Database
- Report Writer
- Absence
- Performance Management
- Recruitment
- Training
- Self Service

6. Timeline and Budget e.g.

The new software must be live and fully operational by June 2021.

The budget set for this project has not yet been settled and approved but should not prove a constraint for the right application

OR

The budget set for this project has been set at £ to include operation for five years after implementation date.

7. Main questions - Use to extract more detailed information on functions and features of particular concern to the organisation e.g.

Please confirm whether your HR & Payroll system can produce payslips at any required frequency and has the capability to run multiple payrolls with different pay dates.

Does your HR & Payroll system provide a leave/absence recording & management functionality (incorporating Holiday absence, Sickness absence & other absences)?

If yes, please describe its functionality, and comment specifically upon:

- Recording different types of absence, combination between unpaid and paid

- Can the system record absence entitlement?

- Is there a reducing Holiday entitlement capability?

We currently use 23 different work and shift patterns; can this number be configured in your system?

Can your HR & payroll system deal with multi-post (where an employee has 2 or more posts on differing service conditions) and record and process absence information for each post?

Do all the other modules integrate with Self service (employee & manager)?

The responses to each point should address the organisation's outlined requirements in detail, describing how the respondent's product and service will meet those requirements. Where a requirement is not met fully, any suggested remedy if feasible.

Where necessary, you can illustrate your questions with extracts from the process maps in order that the vendor can follow what is required.

8. **Supplier Information Required**

    - A brief history of the organisation.

    - Details of any ultimate Holding Company or Investment backing;

    - Addresses of its Registered Office and other business premises;

    - Organisational chart;

    - Contact details for all respondent's employees to be associated with the contract;

    - Web address;

    - Name and address of Bankers;

    - Copies of published and audited accounts for the past three financial years, together with Directors' Reports;

9. **Supplier's Technical Specification - a detailed overview of the application's technical configuration and requirements, including:**

- Platform

- Hardware

- Software

- Broadband capacity

- System performance

- Technical knowledge required and any other relevant factors.

- Highlight all areas where the current technical environment as outlined previously does not correspond or may need to be reviewed in the light of the respondent's application requirements.

10. **Costs - Supply a schedule with each module or stage clearly itemised and accompanied by price indicators.**

These will be some of the typical costs encountered:

- Licences

- Software (including third party applications)

- Possible Customisation – daily costs

- Supplementary Hardware

- Set-Up Costs (costs of vendor's personnel for configuring the software and possible hosting)

- Data Migration (from old system or extracts, on to new system)

- Project Management (also known as consultancy – the daily costs of the vendor's consultant on site information gathering information, liaising with the client and overseeing configuration)

- System Maintenance (annual upgrades both statutory and optional)

- User Training (usually expressed per day per user)

- Support Level Options (where applicable)

- Interface to General Ledger (where applicable, export of data – usually payroll – to the general ledger in the Finance system.

- Any Other Recurring or Non-Recurring Charges

11. Implementation

A specimen Project Plan with time scales and responsibility allocations should accompany the tender document, together with details of:

- Implementation approach and Project Management methodology to be deployed;

- Quality Assurance standards, approach and any Quality accreditations;

- How the respondent's Project personnel will interact with your own project personnel, taking into account their various roles and responsibilities;

- An appreciation of resources, both persons and other physical and fiscal assets that will be required by the client to perform their part of the project;

- Contingency planning in the event of project setback.

12. Evidence of Capacity to Deliver Contract Requirements

Provision of:

- Case studies of the organisation's previous experience of dealing with similar contracts (particular attention should be given to ensure that these studies are relevant, relating to equivalent local authority or public sector clients, and contracts of a similar size).

- Reference sites of comparable sector and size, together with contact details of personnel at those sites.

- Contact details of the application's User Group.

- Details of Escrow arrangements that may exist in respect of the software. This basically holds a copy of the software in trust for the client in the event of failure of the vendor company;

- In the event that sub-contracting likely to be involved, confirmation and evidence that any necessary indemnity has been requested and complied with.

13. Terms & Conditions

A copy of the organisation's standard trading terms and conditions should accompany the response to this invitation.

14. Service Level Agreement

A Draft Service Level Agreement, covering administrational operational and other services to be provided by the tendering organisation to XYZ must be submitted with the response to this Invitation.

15. Management of the tender process

Delivery of Tenders – How many copies, In what format and to whom and where they should be addressed;

Tender timetable:

- to arrive not later than xx hrs. (xx a.m./p.m) local time on day/month/year

- tenders that are delivered late will be returned unopened

- tenders will be opened at xx hours on date / year. Only XYZ staff assigned to this procurement process will be present at the opening of tenders.

- dates set aside for provider presentations

- contract award date

- where and to whom queries should be addressed.

16. Selection criteria – the basis for awarding the contract:

This contract will be awarded on criteria agreed by the relevant authorised personnel at the client, based on their scores for, e.g.:

- functionality
- support service
- quality assurance
- running costs
- technical merit
- relevant client experience
- delivery timetable
- any other relevant matters.

Tendering summary

- do develop a tender process if it works for you. It's not compulsory, but it will help focus you on the acquisition of the right software.

- include practical instances of how your key HR /Payroll processes work, so that vendors can see if their software can do the job

- highlight particular areas that are giving your organisation pain right now and where your processes could be considered unusual

- be realistic with the timelines

- don't produce a gigantic tender document; the vendor needs time

- don't assume demos can be set up with a day's notice – they can't. Give vendors plenty of time to accommodate your programme.

A specimen custom Tendering document is shown in Appendix One, which can be used as a guide or template.

Analysing responses

All of the above points that require a response can be numbered and tabulated, ready for, perhaps, 3 possible answers: Yes, No and Possibly or Partially. "Must have" items must be specially highlighted. A fragment of what that document could look like is shown at Fig 10.

Vendor Response Sheet

Vendor: ABCD

Section 12: Evidence of Capacity to Deliver Contract Requirements

Item	Y	N	Possibly/Partially	Notes
Relevant case studies provided	Y			3 case studies
Reference sites and	Y			4 reference sites
Contact details				
User group and	Y			Details on file
Contact details				
Escrow ?			P	Can be arranged if necessary
Sub-contractors?		N		None used

Fig.11: Vendor response Summary Sheet

Your tenders or enquiries will draw a number of responses from potential vendors, and so the responses to your questions, the detailed specification for each vendor product, and the general information requested will need to be collated and scored according to your own priorities.

Along with this data there will be a schedule of charges and anticipated charges, the latter being estimates by vendors, based on their experience of organisations similar to yours, of the areas that are still undefined such as number of project days, configuration and testing.

The first thing to bear in mind is that most suppliers have their own particular business model. There will therefore be a certain amount of work to do to try to present the complete picture in an understandable format, both to you and the sponsors of the project.

My preferred method is to gather up all the elements of the quotations and lay them out in a way that will show the costs of ownership of the software over a 5 year period. The main elements will consist of:

- Acquisition plan. The usual options are outright purchase, rental, leasing, licensing or subscription based on numbers.

- Annual costs of upgrading (statutory or system related) and / or system maintenance.

- Hosting on vendor's server. This is an option, and will depend very much if you want to host your software on your own premises or not.

- Training staff on system. There will be a training plan for both users and for system administrators. Make sure that you don't try to cut corners on this.

- Project consultancy charges. This will be made up of daily charges for the vendor's consultant both on site to work with the client, and at the vendor's premises working on the agreed configuration.

- Data migration. Again, this is very much an option. Most data migration is done by importing a series of formatted spreadsheets into the system, and over the years I have seen some amazing quotations for this work.

If your data is accurate and current, and you have the in house capability to do it, ask for the templates to be populated, and either the procedure for importing, or agree to send the spreadsheets to the vendor for upload. This is dealt with in Chapter Fifteen.

	Year 1	Year 2	Year 3	Year 4	Year 5	Total
Vendor A						
Rental	20,000	20,000	20,000	20,000	20,000	100,000
Annual Maint.	5,000	5,000	5,000	5,000	5,000	25,000
Training	3,000	-	-	-	-	3,000
Hosting	8,000	8,000	8,000	8,000	8,000	40,000
Project costs	35,000	-	-	-	-	35,000
	71,000	33,000	33,000	33,000	33.000	
Total cost of ownership						203,000
Vendor B						
Rental	24,000	24,000	24,000	24,000	24,000	
Annual Maint.	5,000	5,000	5,000	5,000	5,000	
Training	included	-	-	-	-	
Hosting	7,500	7,500	7,500	7,500	7,500	
Project costs	32,000	-	-	-	-	

	68,500	36,500	36,500	36,500	36,500	
Total cost of ownership						214,500

Fig.12 Costs of ownership of HRIS

In Fig.12 you will see part of an actual analysis done during a live project. Apart from the cost variations for each element, you will notice that Vendor B did not charge for the training. On the basis that there is no such thing as a free lunch, that cost would probably have been aggregated in the rental, but this does show why you need to set things out and think in terms of total ownership expenditure.

Many organisations will sink the project costs as a one-off item and capitalise them, so that they may not be considered in the 5 year costs.

Don't be afraid to ask after any other costs that may not have been included in the schedule submitted by the vendor. It is very unlikely that there are any, but it does no harm to double check.

CHAPTER 13

THE SELECTION PROCESS

The approach to selection needs careful consideration to avoid the all-too-common trap of being dazzled by offers that turn out to be elegant and sexy solutions to problems that you don't actually have, while at the same time overlooking the very products that you actually need.

Product Demonstrations

At the end of this book I have given a summary of the five major minefields that will derail – or seriously damage - your project. The product demonstration is one of them.

The product demonstration will constitute the greater part of the decision-making process in the acquisition of HR & payroll systems and is therefore the area most likely where the wrong decisions are going to be made. And they have been!

Why? People like to see "whizzy" features, and being cosseted by potential vendors, and for a space in time are in a position to dictate. It is the "sexy" part of sourcing HRIS, going to product shows, and talking to vendors, and in a number of cases has actually been the starting point for the project without much aforethought.

Over the past few years, the number of integrated HR & Payroll providers has remained fairly static, while the number of specialist or single purpose applications (e.g. HR, e-Recruitment, Talent Management) has slowly continued to grow.

As most of these types of software tick many of the same boxes, and software as a product continues to look standard (intuitive for most users of social media), the prospective buyer must work harder to identify the key factors that differentiate between them.

The demonstration has to be well put together or it will be a waste of time; the secret to a meaningful demonstration lies in the amount of preparation we have done from the previous modules. It must be scripted - and you have to drive the complete agenda.

Some purchasers like to spring questions on presenting vendors, others don't: it's all a matter of preferred style. My own preference is for the prospect to raise the key areas of concern beforehand, so that the vendor can be equipped to answer comprehensively. Nothing is so frustrating for all concerned if the visiting team have to refer back to someone at base, probably not until the next day.

So what should a product demonstration actually achieve? I see it as the end point of a lot of preliminary hard work aimed at yielding measurable evidence of which software products can be considered to be fit for the organisation's purpose. It focuses on problems you need to solve and processes and procedures that may be complex.

When asking the demonstrator questions on usage, make sure that they demonstrate how it is done. It is natural for a salesman to say 'yes we can", and, indeed, most of the time that's true, but there are occasions when the actual doing is a lot more complex in practice.

Listen out for answers that indicate that customisation will be required, or that a certain feature will be available 'at next release'. Make sure that you are satisfied that this is not a grey area that will cause you problems later on.

Remember - the presence of a module in the software does NOT mean that it can be configurable to your needs. This needs to be demonstrated.

There are three main types of product demonstrations:

- Exhibitions
- In house and
- Online

The locations and ambience may differ, but there are a number of factors that they all have in common:

- The correct people must be present

- The demonstration format must be tightly scripted by the potential client (you)

- Each demonstration must be scored on a consistent basis

- Every vendor should be accorded equal conditions.

Exhibitions

Let's see if this picture is familiar.

You arrive at the exhibition hall at opening time of after a gruelling 2 hour+ journey through the rush hour. You are tired already, and so grab an exhibition guide at the door and head for the refreshment area for coffee and a pastry.

Whilst you refresh yourself, you flick through the guide, and – because you have done little or no preparation - mark maybe five vendors that you think are worth visiting.

You set off for the first stand, where you are eagerly received, and – again – because you have nothing particular in mind, you ask to see a walk-through of the software, provoking a 40 minute session of the most mind-blowing thing you have ever seen. Naturally, the vendor will show you the best parts.

You leave your details and take some brochures, stuffing them into the bag so thoughtfully provided, and any other freebies on offer and head for the next one on your list.

The second demonstration takes a little less time than the first one, because you are asking questions that arise from comparing with the first product, and perhaps this software doesn't look as good as the first. Or was it the salesperson's presentation skills? In any case, you are not quite convinced.

Taking your leave of vendor number 2, you look for the third stand. It is now quarter to twelve, the hall is filling up and getting stuffy and noisy and your feet are hot. You arrive at the third targeted stand, and, drawing on your experiences at the first two, start to ask to see specific areas of this vendor's software. By after midday, you have the brochures from this vendor, and so head back to the refreshment area for a sandwich and a cold drink.

During the break, looking at the brochures and any hastily jotted notes, you feel that product number 1 was probably more or less the same as product number 3, and that product 2 is not as good. You revisit the guide. You have just about had enough at looking at flashing screens, so decide on a new tactic: pick up brochures from the two you haven't seen yet, and, for good measure, from 3 others that you have now marked in the guide, so that you can study them at leisure on the way home.

You now have a mission. Walking down the middle of the aisles to avoid being accosted by random salespeople, you drop into each of the five other stands for a quick conversation, exchange of visiting cards and brochures for the bag (that is now getting heavy).

3.45 pm and you are now feeling pretty weary. It has to be time to go to beat the rush hour, and at least you can say that you have covered eight products!

The next day there is some early-breaking crisis washing over HR (probably because you were out for the day before), so the exhibition material gets filed for now, to be reviewed later. An informal report will be drawn up on the evidence of the 2 point something actual demonstrations and the brochure material, pointing the way forward for the acquisition of new HR software. With luck the IT people will pick up on anything that is remiss with the products.

This is all very familiar to me from my early days of looking at systems, and to all of my practitioner colleagues, and yet, amazing as it may seem, many HRIS purchase decisions are made largely on the strength of what was perceived on that day.

How can we do this right in the future?

Let's assume that you have done all the homework specified in this book: process maps, required software specification, process scenarios and highlighted areas of "pain" in your current operation.

First, you must do research beforehand; go to the exhibition website and see who is exhibiting there, and then compare the offers on their own individual sites to see if they broadly line up with what is in your specification. A site such as HRcomparison can help you compare between up to 5 vendors at a time.

Book an appointment with the stand at a specific time, for no more than an hour's duration. Introduce yourself as someone who is looking seriously at the market, and send on a couple of your scenarios, asking for them to be demonstrated in real time. At this point, you could ask for some general information as to price and implementation time.

Hash out a score sheet based on the points you want to see met as you will need these later.

If at all possible, if your journey is long, try to travel down the night before. Yes, there is a cost to this, but you are going to be party to a large investment decision, and it pays to arrive fresh.

Be punctual, out of respect to the vendor, who has paid out a lot of money for their stand. It helps if you have been assigned a specific salesperson beforehand. Take brochures and other collateral that is available, and business cards, and try to establish who should be the follow-up point of contact if required.

If there's one thing a vendor really likes, and will respond favourably to, it is a qualified lead, i.e. someone who is in the market and knows what they want to see. Their nightmare is a person who shows up at the stand unannounced and asks "so what does your software do?"

Don't try to see more than four vendors in the day using this methodology; it is tiring, and you will need to be concentrating even more on evaluating than if it were an unscripted presentation. The major shows go on for a couple of days, so if you have six or seven you want to see, take another overnight to clear your head and begin again.

When you return to base with your sheets showing how well the various vendors have coped with your questioning, you can then draw up a matrix of results and assign scores, to indicate who should be on a long or short list.

Of course, not all software vendors exhibit at these shows, so you will still need to do the research so that no stone is left unturned. These vendors may be able to offer an online demonstration.

In house

In house demonstrations (demos) are usually held as a follow-up to an earlier viewing, probably at an exhibition.

Assuming that these demos are is as a follow-up of interest in a system seen elsewhere, you now have to plan this very carefully.

The first thing I would like to point out is that I favour a two demo approach; the content for each I shall discuss a bit further on. I prefer to see as much as I can of this product that can possibly cost the purchaser a serious amount of money, and I would not care to base any recommendation at one good sitting.

The following factors are key to safeguarding a successful outcome:

- Location
- Equipment
- Attendees
- Duration
- Subject matter
- Evaluation

Location

The size will depend on number of attendees, but must facility the comfort of your audience and demonstrators. I have sat in on demos where the visiting team literally melted before our very eyes; others where the zeal for air conditioning not only numbed the senses of people of the room, but the constant background noise induced a sort of hypothermic torpor.

Choose a space that is light and airy, and you can guarantee attention. Try to break your audience into groups rather than a cinema style seating arrangement, and if these groups can be related (e.g. HR, payroll, IT, finance) it makes post-discussion easier.

Equipment

Ask the vendor beforehand what they may require to be present, and what they may be bringing; there is a plethora of presentational equipment available, so check carefully what may be needed.

A reliable internet connection is almost de rigueur nowadays, so make sure it is running and allows access to your visitors. Don't wait till the same morning to talk to your IT department, have it set up and running beforehand.

Attendees

Let's start by finding out how many from the vendor team will be present, and what each role will be. This can vary from two up to seven.

As for the "home" team, this is very much up to the prospective purchaser.

We have sat in on presentations with audiences from two to 22, and can say that the more people, the slower everything goes.

Overall, it is recommended that the key sponsor(s) is present, together with those personnel concerned with the strategic implications of the application, and key users who will be expected to make it work on a tactical level.

People I feel should be there are:

First demo:

- The project sponsor

- Senior HR team

- Senior payroll representative (if applicable)

- A senior finance representative (especially if interfacing with general ledger)

- An IT representative. IT has an involvement, of course, but with software developments nowadays, they may now be focusing more on the specification and maintenance of environments and peripheral applications such as Internet Explorer and MS Office. Single sign on is also a particular concern.

- Any others who politically need to be involved, also known as "key influencers". They are there on a "need to know" basis rather than assist selection.

I have deliberately opted for seniors at this stage, as the first viewing tends to be rather more strategic in content.

Second demo:

As for the first demo, plus the complete HR and payroll teams. The "political" visitor may not be necessary if they feel sufficiently involved already.

Any internal "customer" who may be affected by the operation of new software.

It's probably not worth dragging your Procurement people along to demonstrations– their enquiries can be more effectively handled offline.

Duration

Demos are attention intensive, and remember that you will be allocating points for the whole time. Ideally the first one should last no more than 2 – 2.5 hours, the second somewhat longer, perhaps to a maximum of 3.5 hours.

It is crucial that each vendor should have the same time allocation. Be strict on when to call time, even if the vendor is in full flow – they have not used their time effectively.

Do not attempt to encompass more than two demonstrations in a day, otherwise it's just too much to take in.

Subject matter

My aim in the first demonstration is to get a "look and feel" of the software and address functionality and configurability in crucial areas. The second is to drill in on key processes in more detail, and talk about ancillaries such as timelines, project approach, and next steps.

In good time before each demo, the vendors should be circulated with our agenda for the session, together with samples of scenarios that are either causing pain currently, or involve processes slightly out of the ordinary. (Most organisations like to contend that they are unique, but this is not necessarily true in the majority of cases). Sending them dummy or anonymised data to use will ensure consistency in what we will expect to see.

Start with a 5 minute section on the vendor and its history, and then perhaps a similar time for an overview of the technical environment.

Move on to look at the landing page (can it be configured both for organisational branding, and then for employee individuality?), menus and navigational features, and then typical screens such as an employee record or a sample absence report.

It may sound absurd, but you will need to check that the software can handle your employee numbering system, and generate sequential numbers going forward. Unless, that is, you choose to go completely revise the numbering.

Using data already supplied, you can then move on to routine transactions such as inputting a new employee, paying them, running a payslip, giving them a pay rise, recording absence and terminating them.

According to your script - and using more sample data and process charts previously supplied, they can then demonstrate how to compile a work flow, a triggered (automated) action, reports, organisation charts and audit trails.

Following on from this is the part where your scenarios are addressed, and I show some examples in Appendix Three to give an idea of their construction. These scenarios should be derived from your processes maps, and be directly related to problem areas that you currently have. They should be constructed in such a way that you can identify whether or not the need you have is going to be met by the demonstrated software.

Do not accept any "ready-made" solutions to your queries such as a report all ready to run. It is the step-by-step assembly of the solution to your scenarios that will show whether or not it works with your process, and whether your own users perceive it to be one with which they can work..

Evaluation

You will need to devise a scoring system for your team to use when attending demonstrations, and this will depend very much on what your priorities are. For simplicity's sake, you could show three levels of completion, e.g.

Item No.	Status	Score
	Not demonstrated	0
	Demonstrated – partially meets requirements	5
	Fully meets requirements	10

If a vendor shows you some wonderful feature that you have not specified, then NO points are awarded, and they are, in effect, burning the time allowed to them. Remind them if that, if necessary.

Note that different parties may require different scoring factors; for instance, your users may be more interested in ease of use, clean navigation and fewer screens and key strokes to perform routine activities, whereas strategic staff will be looking at report building capabilities. Accordingly, design different score sheets for each group.

Key features can be assigned a priority weighting, according to their importance to the organisation.

Remember, if you are scoring over a lengthy demonstration, the attention span will be fully stretched, so arrange for breaks at convenient times to refresh mind and body!

Sheets must be completed either during or just after the demo, while the memory is fresh.

You will notice in the example score sheet at fig 13 that certain criteria such as multicurrency, single sign on and audit trail or missing. These factors are straightforward, and will have been used either in the initial filtering of applicants to your tender, or during your initial researches. You will be focusing more on the capability – and flexibility - of the application to cope with your processes.

			Software A	Software B	Software C
Topic	Scoring range	Maximum Score	Actual	Actual	Actual
Front end branding for organisation	0-10	10	8	8	9
Home page individualisation	0-10	10	8	9	9
Ease of configuring fields	0-20	20	16	14	16
Ease of navigation	0-10	10	10	10	9
User face acceptability	0-10	10	9	7	8
Workflow example	0-20	20	17	16	18
Automated (triggered) action example	0-20	20	20	16	18
Headcount report example	0-20	20	14	16	16
Absence example	0-20	20	15	15	15
Organisation charting	0-20	20	13	15	17

	Scoring range	Maximum Score	Software A	Software B	Software C
Topic			Actual	Actual	Actual
Totals		160	130 (81%)	126 (79%)	135 (84%)

Fig.13 Demonstration scoresheet

Notice the weighting of points allocated is inclined more towards the software demonstrating its ability to cope with the specific examples. This will vary according to organisational requirements.

It is probably best to restrict the list of topics to a workable number, as the need to rate too many aspects will hamper attempts to actually watch the demonstration!

Online Demonstrations

The agenda and preparation of material for an online demo is essentially the same for an in house one, but unless you have a very big screen, you may need to restrict the numbers taking part.

Furthermore, watching a small screen can quickly become very tiring, so try limit the duration to no more than one and a half hours.

It is preferable to have a live demonstration at some point of the decision process

I would mention here one other option, and that is trying out a demo copy of the HRIS software. This is a very popular approach with smaller vendors, but you will need to invest a considerable amount of time to populate it in order to test it in a meaningful way.

Don't forget to thank the vendor for their time; they will have invested a lot of time to organise their demonstration to your specification, and may have travelled a long distance to get to you. Courtesy costs nothing – and is everything.

Finally, I just want to reinforce my earlier message: first define the features you require, and then establish that those features can be configured to match your needs. If you keep this at the forefront, you won't go very far wrong.

CHAPTER 14

THE DECISION

In a world where many products can superficially appear to homogenous, there won't necessarily be a clear-cut path to arriving at a conclusion. Review the facts as you have them, and DON'T always be swayed by price. If you have identified a genuine business need, then cost should not be the primary driver.

You now have the projected costs, and the score sheets from your demo rounds. After merging all the results, it is now time to decide.

As we have said before, there is probably no 'perfect fit' for you; as with most things in life, there is always a compromise, unless you are prepared to spend a lot of money customising the product. Customisation can, in many cases, indicate that a particular existing process is being replicated on the new technology, and I would strongly advise you not to go down that road.

If none of the products you see come close to meeting what you see to be your requirements, then you need to re-examine your criteria. In my opinion, the only things that most modern software cannot cope with are cumbersome and / or illogical processes, and you need to ask yourself if you really need to be doing them. Have another look at them.

As part of your decision making, here are some extra factors to throw into the pot:

1. Implementation time

Prospective customers are now increasingly looking at an area that up till now has been the source of much pain in terms of time and cost: the implementation phase.

Traditionally, project estimates have been excessive and implementation times and consultancy days stretched to the limits of credibility. Of course, there was at least one reason for this: to allow for the unsuspected problems lurking within the client's processes and data structures.

Nevertheless, clients were saddled with high charges for importation of data into the new application, and the ill-prepared ones paid a tough penalty in the form of consultant charges to put their own data, rules and hierarchies into an order ready for introduction to the software.

Organisations no longer have the luxury of time or money to sustain extravagant project times and costs; advances in technology and greater user expectation demand a speedier approach. It stands to reason that if vendors can bring down project duration, the client pays for less consultation time, has less charge on its internal resources, and vendors are able to utilise the gain in extra capacity to service yet more customers.

In order to address this market trend, some vendors will have to change their mind set; a medium-sized company will be looking to deploy within weeks rather than months and vendors who meet this agility challenge will be the winners. This is a worthwhile aspiration for any player in the current market place, and there is no reason why it cannot be achieved. Of course, the fly in the ointment has always been the state of readiness of the prospective client

2. Should we have the same HR and payroll provider?

My answer would almost always be yes. Despite having heard plenty of "best of breed" arguments over the years, having to link two discrete systems just stores up a lot of cost and headaches for years to come.

3. Make sure your product is future proof:

Don't select a product that has been patched over and re-skinned for the last 12 years. It's like those cars they used to sell with a nice body, full of extras, but built on an outmoded floor pan.

4. Functions and features matching your list don't mean it can do the job for you:

It's all in the configuration. Yes, you've heard it before – often – but this really is the key.

5. How much will this cost?

Value for money is the best way to go, but don't be too obsessed with the budget. Better to look for the closest fit and then make the figures work. You've identified this project as a business priority, now go in to bat for the money using the case that you built.

6. Service levels

Service levels don't loom as large as they used to if you opt for vendor hosting. Amendments and adjustments can be carried out at the vendor site. Fundamentally, they need to make sure that your connection to the software is kept running 24/7, that they comply with statutory updates in a timely fashion, and that your data is secure and backed up in case of emergency.

7. Reference sites

Reference sites are customers whose experience with the vendor has been a happy one. Did they get it right? Did they throw a wad of money at the issue to make it work? Did the vendor move Heaven and earth to make it work so they could have a success story? Cynical, of course. If you take up with reference sites, make sure that the questions you ask drill right in to what you need to know.

Is the organisation comparable to your own? How was it configured? How long to install? And so on.

8. User Groups

An active user group will always encourage a vendor to develop their product. Ask for an introduction to chat to one or more of the most prominent members of that group, to get an idea of what current issues there may be, and where the software appears to be heading.

9. Negotiate…

…but not to the extent that the vendor will be looking to economise in other areas of your deal, once the deal is signed. Appearing macho to your colleagues for grinding the supplier into the dust is all very well, but things work much better when that supplier is working to please the client rather than trying to subsist on a rock bottom price. In business, mutual benefit works best.

10. Chemistry!

Nothing you will be able to put on a spreadsheet, of course, but you need to have a consensus about who you feel most comfortable dealing with. People's instincts are actually rarely wrong. You want to be dealing with a vendor who is flexible, supportive and creative in offering solutions to your problems, and – importantly – will have a person assigned to you to ensure that the relationship develops over time. Fortunately, we are now in the era of sustainable business, and the better vendors have recognised this.

Below is an outline of an actual plan for an organisation of over 6,000 employees that I drew up, having evaluated their "state of readiness". They were obliged, as a matter of policy, to undergo the full tendering process.

Here you will see from a standing start they were able to get to a decision in 8 months. Of course, a smaller or perhaps even a more agile organisation can arrive at that point a lot faster, but thoroughness at the beginning of the project is rewarded many times over later on.

Task	Months							
	1	2	3	4	5	6	7	8
Form project team	█							
Issue PQQ (pre-qualifying questionnaire)	█							
PQQ responses & processing		█						
Data Cleanse	█	█	█					
Hierarchy validation	█	█	█					
Process reviews	█	█	█					
Confirm functions and features			█					
Confirm reporting suite			█					
Compile tender collateral			█	█				
Issue tender					█			
Tender responses & processing					█	█		
Invitation to Demo 1						█		
Invitation to Demo 2							█	
Investigations (reference sites, etc.)							█	█
Decision								█

Fig 14 Projected timeline plan

And just one more thing…

….HR Directors and Managers select it, but HR and payroll administration staff have to use it; those sexy and esoteric features that you saw slickly demonstrated at a software exhibition may prove tricky to use in an operational context. Listen to what your habitual users have to say about the products.

CHAPTER 15

THE PROJECT PLAN

The selected vendor will supply you with a road map for implementation in the form of the project plan. You will need to interpret the plan with regard to understanding what this means in terms of your resources and organisational timetable, as well as the responsibilities devolving to each side.

Once the decision is made, your project is very much live and into the implementation stage.

We have already discussed the advisability of having one's own project manager (PM), and it is at this point that they start to earn their keep. Although, as HR and payroll professionals, we will not be directly managing the project, it is important that we understand what is happening along the way.

It is usual for the Vendor to draw up a project plan detailing the actions required to load, configure, implement and test the application up to purchaser acceptance and sign-off. Areas of responsibility for the client will be clearly identified, as well as a projected timeline with milestones. These are stages 1 and 2 on the project plan shown in Fig.15 which is derived from a real-life one for a client of just over 1000 employees.

For the sake of space and clarity, I have compressed and simplified it but it shows clearly the sense of task, responsibility and time.

As the client, you will need to draw up a mirror plan that will comprise all the steps to be taken from your side, the persons responsible for resourcing those steps and the timelines for those steps to accord with the Vendor plan.

Be sure to contact your vendor well beforehand to check what data, rules and documentation will need to be ready and to hand for the consultant. Additionally, make sure that your internal people are available and can spend the required time with consultants while they are information gathering in the early stages.

If you do not have (expensive) Project planning software tools for this, you can draw up your chart in Gantt format using MS Excel.

No	Task	Resp.	Weeks															
			1	2	3	4	5	6	7	8	9	10	11	12	13	14	15	16
1	Project plan development	Vendor	▓	▓	▓													
2	Project plan agreement	Client				▓												
3	Establish test environments	Client		▓														
4	Application configuration	Vendor			▓	▓	▓											
5	Preparation & migration of data	Client/Vendor						▓										
6	Load & first test of static data	Client/Vendor							▓									
7	User acceptance of loaded data	Client/Vendor								▓								
8	First test environment run	Client/Vendor									▓							
9	Second test environment run	Client/Vendor										▓						
12	First parallel run	Client/Vendor											▓					

No	Task	Resp.	Weeks															
			1	2	3	4	5	6	7	8	9	10	11	12	13	14	15	16
13	Reconciliation & correction of 1st parallel run	Client													▓			
14	Second parallel run	Client/ Vendor														▓		
15	Reconciliation & correction of 2nd parallel run	Client															▓	
	Acceptance & Go live	Client																▓

Fig.15: Vendor project plan

110

CHAPTER 16

CONFIGURATION

Configurability is King in the modern HRIS software arena, to ensure that the product is going to work specifically to your operational requirements. The detail for this will draw upon the processes and rules that you gathered at the very beginning of this project.

In the preliminary stages leading up to selection, you may have been able to map out some of the stages relating to triggered actions and work flow, based on your processes and procedures. If so, then well done! But I suspect that most of you would have been extremely tied up just mapping processes, procedures and tabulating rules. Here we will look in more detail at the various elements of configuration that will need to be done.

For better clarity, I have deliberately avoided technical jargon, as this is intended as a guide for the practitioner, not the implementers.

A. Organisational Structure

Although the structure will be in our Rules material that we assembled while the selection process was under way, each division, department and other groups will need to be numbered. Our recommended action here is to replicate the organisation structure numbering on the basis of the Chart of Accounts used by the Finance Department. Not only does it make the reporting understandable across the organisation, but it facilitates the smooth export of information to other applications.

Departments can be configured to carry the numeric chart number as well as an alpha description (e.g. department 000912: Credit Control Department).

When setting up the structure, remember to have the organisation itself at the top of the "pyramid" otherwise you will not be able to transit people between departments.

(See Figure 4: Organisational Structure Page **)

B. The front end

Many software vendors now give their clients options for customising or configuring the appearance of the application.

The main option is to have the primary page with the client logo, graphics and colours. This will be done by the vendor in consultation with the client.

Additionally, there is the capability for each user to configure their primary page, enabling them to show messages, reminders and certain key rolling data in a "dashboard" format.

It is possible to present these pages in a more "social media" format, which gain instant recognition from users familiar with those applications.

C. Data fields

Pretty much all software comes with pre-configured fields, so it will be a question of retitling some to match your own usage, adding some which are specific to your organisation, and then defining the format of the content, alpha or numeric only, or alphanumeric, and desired field character length.

Below, I give a sample of the fields most usually required for HR and payroll in the United Kingdom. These will of course vary in nature and syntax throughout global territories, but form the generic core categories of most systems.

HR database fields:
Personal:
Employee Number   Your format e.g. AB001. Allow capacity.
Forenames
Surnames
National Insurance   xx-xx-xx-x
Number
Nationality   pick list

Work Permit	Not required /Yes If Yes, reference number.
Address *see note below*	
Contact Details	telephone / mobile phone/ personal email
Emergency Contact	Full name / relationship /telephone number/s
Date of Continuous Employment	--/--/---- or as required.
Date of Employment in current post	--/--/---- or as required.
Trade Union membership	If Yes, pick list for which union
Educational details	
Professional Qualifications	
Previous employment details	
Company Property (where applicable)	
Date of Leaving	--/--/---- or as required.
Reason for Leaving	pick list
Exit Interview details (for leavers)	
Criminal Records Bureau Check	

Post:

Job Title/s	For control purposes, best from a pick list.
Location	pick list
Probation expiry date	--/--/---- or as required.
Notice required	pick list
Grade	pick list
Full Time / Part Time / Job Share / Multi Post	pick list
Hours of Work	e.g. 35 Can be p.w, p.a. or as required.
Work Pattern	pick list

| Permanent / Temporary/ Contract / Agency/ Casual | pick list |

Reporting to

Service Unit Costing details

Employment History

Compensation:

Salary

Car Car Allowance

Childcare Vouchers

Other Benefits / Allowances

Pension Scheme membership

Equality:

Gender

Date of Birth

Marital Status

Ethnicity

Disability

Religion

Sexual Orientation

Health & Safety:

Accident Details

Eye Tests

First Aider / Fire Marshal / Other

Note that many of the above fields can be configured to offer a pick list (which appears in a drop down box).

A special note about Address fields

As homogeneity of the data and its presentation are essential, we need to force entered data to conform to the rules we wish to apply. Nowhere is this seen more than in Address fields. For clarity, we should present the fields for entry (in UK) in something like the following format:

Name or number of house / apartment	(Alphanumeric)
Building	(Alphanumeric)
Street	(Alphanumeric)
Town	(Alphanumeric)
County	(Alpha)
Postcode	(Alphanumeric / Capitals)

Note that we also have specified what type of characters can be expected in this field, and this will apply to all fields. To save time, most of these will have already been set up in the basic software.

D. **Absence**

Absence encompasses the whole spectrum from Holidays, Maternity/paternity, Compassionate, Unpaid, Obligatory and Illness. Set up as standard in the system will be any public holidays accruing for each year.

It will be necessary to identify which days are normal working days, so that all absences can be computed. In the UK, 4 consecutive days of illness (including non-working days) trigger Statutory Sick Pay.

The basic data applying to any absence are:

- Date of commencement of absence
- Date of termination of absence
- Duration of absence
- Reason for absence.

Will part of a day count as a whole day, or will you divide a day into two parts?

A time & attendance system, of course, would drill down to the minute, recording the clocking in and out of an employee.

Following on from this will be the categories of absence. To keep the configured drop-down boxes from being too unwieldy, I would suggest something along the lines of the following:

Type of absence:

a) Holidays

- Paid
- Unpaid

The first will be deducted on a reducing basis from the annual entitlement of the employee concerned. The second will have an effect on the employee's pay and should generate an entry on the payroll part of the software.

b) Family leave

- Maternity
- Paternity
- Adoption
- Unpaid parental/family leave

The first three will be applied against either the statutory entitlements, or the organisation's own occupational ones. The last will affect the payroll.

c) Public duties
- Jury service
- Other public duties

The treatment of this is at discretion of the employer; they may be paid or unpaid, and a "reasonable" time limit taken into account.

d) Sickness

Here the matter becomes very much more complicated. I would think that the primary concern regarding illness will be whether or not it is deemed to be occupationally-related, so the first filter could be:

- Occupational
- Other

"Occupational" could then offer a selection from the most commonly-occurring incidents in the industry or sector. For instance, in a manufacturing environment, the selection could include, for example:

- Loss or damage to digit/s
- Loss or damage to limb/s
- Injury to torso
- Damage to hearing
- Damage to eyesight

The information from these will be cross-referenced to entries in the Accident Book.

"Other" will encompass all the other possible illness causes, and you will need to be careful that you don't end up with a drop-down box with 1500 items scrolling away into infinity. One way to avoid this is to assign a range of categories such as:

- Breaks & fractures
- Coronary & pulmonary
- Migraines & hay fever
- Colds and influenza

- Infectious disease
- Eyes, ears, nose
- Digestive and intestinal
- Other

Within these, there can be sub-categories, such as:

Breaks & fractures:

- Broken limb
- Fractured limb
- Spinal
- Hip
- Torsal

How these are set up or arranged is very much up to the organisation, how it likes to report its sickness absence, and for what purposes. The important thing is to make it easy to use as far as possible, as when your employees are using self service to report in sick, it's not too clever for them to have to wade through endless selections to find the right one.

These periods of sickness absence will be plotted against the statutory periods of sickness configured in the software, and qualifying periods identified to trigger Statutory Sick Pay in the payroll. Linkage will also be recorded.

If there is an enhanced occupational entitlement, this too will be calculated, and where SSP is exhausted, payment will be automatically terminated.

e)   Career breaks and sabbaticals

These may not necessarily be configured unless there is an organisational policy. If so, then there will be limits, and notice as to whether or not the employee's pay is affected.

Absence recording must be set up so that the organisation can get to the information it needs:

Payroll - so that entitlements can be paid, or deduction effected where appropriate;

Employees – so they can work out what they are being paid;

Management – to identify problem areas of absence (poor management is a significant factor)

E.   Automatic Triggers

To set up triggers, you will need to refer to your process maps. Remember that triggers are activated in response to changes in the data, and so you will need to plan:

- For what process you need to build a trigger;
- What data change will activate it;
- To whom the notifications should be sent;
- By what medium the notification will be sent and
- The actual format and wording of the notification.

Let's look at an example.

In this organisation, all new employees are on a 12 week probation period commencing from the start date, and you want to ensure that the probation interview is carried out on time.

You configure the trigger by ensuring that the Probation rule for this employee is 3 months. You can then set the trigger to forward a formatted and mail merged email reminder to the Line Manager, the employee (and HR department, if necessary) at start date plus, say 10 weeks.

Example:

Trigger	New employee entered on system	HR
Field	Probation	
Condition	Employee start date	
Action	Email	
Message	"Please note that (employee number) (employee name) is due for probation review on (date – derived from start date + 12 weeks). Please ensure that this is completed by the due date and the decision communicated to the employee with a copy to the HR department." (Signature name) (job title)	
Recipients	New employee, manager of new employee, HR department (if required	

Fig 16 Triggered action example

The blank fields are populated in the actual message by a mail merge function.

This is simplistic, but gives an indication of how these Triggers are constructed.

A variation of the trigger is a flag. This will generate a message when a certain condition arises within the database, and they can be developed for complex situations.

A simple example could be to advise when the required number of First Aiders is deficient due to an employee leaving. One way of achieving that would be to schedule a report that runs, say, every day to determine the total of First Aiders. If the required total was 6, then any time that the total falls below that, i.e. is <6, a report or email is sent to a designated person for action.

A more sophisticated one could be to monitor employees who take an exceptional number of Fridays or Mondays off work! This would involve setting up a report that looks at absence days equalling Friday, or Monday, or both. If those days total more than a given number, then the report or an email are sent to the relevant persons.

Triggers and flags can be set up to send SMS messages as well, if required.

F.   Payroll fields

In your preparatory work you will probably have reviewed the fields that you are currently using in payroll, and calculated how many spares you may need for future expansion, as part of the requirements for your potential vendor.

Pay Elements e.g.:

Salary (monthly)
Overtime
Bonus
Sickness absence pay (Statutory and Occupational)
Holiday pay
Maternity and Paternity leave pay
Expenses (where paid through the payroll)
Pay items that attract National Insurance / Social Security
Pay items that are exempt from NI / Social Security
Taxable and non-taxable elements

Deduction Elements e.g.

Income Tax deducted at source
National insurance / Social Security
Pensions
Additional Voluntary Pension contributions
Social club membership
Medical insurance contribution
Company loans for sundry purposes
Union dues
Other voluntary subscriptions
Deductions due to court orders

These elements should have the ability to be used for:

Permanent and temporary arrangements
Taxable and non-taxable definitions
Pensionable and non-pensionable definitions
User defined arithmetic and conditional calculations
Validation controls
The fields will be cumulative (e.g. pay, tax and contributions) or reducing balance (e.g. loans and court orders) or neither, and can be cleared down at the end of every month if required.
Ideally, payroll fields should use the same references as those set down in the chart of accounts* to facilitate transfer of bulk or other data to the general

---

*   *The chart of accounts is a complete listing of every account in an accounting system. An account is a unique record for each type of asset, liability, equity, revenue and expense. Each of these accounts will bear a unique code number, and it is these code numbers that should be mirrored in the payroll fields.*

Within the categories of operating revenues and expenses, accounts might be further organised by business function, e.g. Production, Sales, HR, Facilities, Finance and Management or by Divisions and Locations, which you will see can more or less follow the organisation chart of an enterprise. Within those headings will be a host of sub-accounts such as salaries, expenses, premises overheads, heat, light and power, and so on.

The chart of accounts can be as large as the organisation requires it to be, and big international corporations will have incredible complexity (and a commensurate number of accountants!) whereas a small company will probably want to operate a very basic structure.

ledger* For example, if the Sales department is shown as S019 in the chart of accounts, this number should appear as a cost centre on the HR & payroll system.

G. e-recruitment / Applicant tracking

e-recruitment is designed to automate processes as much as possible, and therefore we need to harness its capabilities to the full.

Once approved, job vacancies can be posted to the organisation's website or job board via a portal. This makes these posts available for application both internally and externally.

If desired, pre-qualifying questions can filter the applications down to those most relevant to requirements, such as:

"A degree in engineering from a recognised body is required for this post. Can you confirm that you have this? Y / N". "No" triggers an immediate rejection.

"Can you confirm that you are legally permitted to work in this country? Y/N"

Likewise rejected with a "No" response.

Responses can be automatically launched both to the unsuccessful candidates, and to those moving to the next stage.

Applications are then routed direct to the hiring manager, who on review will select some for interview and the rest to be advised of non-success.

Interviews can be scheduled, with their outcomes also handled through the response process. For successful one, a more personalised communication is recommended.

A simplified diagram is shown in Fig.17

* *The general ledger is the whole record – usually arranged in accounting periods and financial years – of the financial transactions of an organisation. From this source are prepared all the operational, financial and statutory statements that are required to be produced.*

STAGE	ACTION	RESPONSIBLE			
1	Approved vacancy posted to website/ job board	Recruitment or hiring manager			
2.	Applicant applies	Applicant			
				Fails filter	Rejection and end of application
			▶	Passes filter	Application forwarded
3	Application reviewed	Hiring manager			
				Passed	Inteview communication
			▶	Fail	Rejection communication
4	Interview	Hiring manager			
				Fail	Rejection communication
			▶	Hire decision	Success advice
5	Offer	HR			Offer and Contract

Fig.17 e-recruitment work flow

All candidate details are stored for the recommended period and can be reported on. The online application form will be designed to meet all requirements and will include equal opportunity monitoring details.

This type of software is nearly always comes with a wide range of branding options and is easily configured to mirror the processes required by the organisation.

H.   Recruitment Administration

This module differs from e-recruitment in that although you can use your website or job boards to attract candidates, the way they are handled is not so automatic.

Looking at the work flow in Fig. 17, you will see that communications to the candidates are manually generated from the system, using templates. Likewise, the organisation of interviews has rather more manual intervention as well.

STAGE	ACTION	RESPONSIBLE	
1	Approved vacancy posted to website/job board	Recruitment or hiring manager	
2.	Applicant applies	Applicant	
3	Applicant details entered on Recruitment admin module	Recruitment or HR	Acknowledgement of receipt (mail merged from module)
4.	Application passed to hiring manager	Recruitment or HR	
5	Application reviewed and short list chosen	Hiring manager	
6	Responses to candidates	Recruitment or HR	Interview dates for successful; Rejections for unsuccessful. (mail merged)
7	Interviews	Hiring manager	
8	Decision	Hiring manager	
9	Communication	Recruitment or HR	Rejections for unsuccessful.
10	Offer	HR	Offer and Contract

Fig.18 Recruitment administration work flow

This module certainly has its uses, but would probably be suited to a smaller organisation with a moderately low level of recruitment activity. Certainly if you are recruiting 50 or more posts a year, you should consider the investment in e-recruitment.

I.   Reports

You will have to think about the variety of reports to which you will need access from the outset, what fields should appear, how they are to be filtered and if there are any time or departmental parameters. These can be used in the Report writing Training sessions, as there is no substitute in learning as doing these things for yourself!

Some reports use the same building blocks and only needed to be modified, perhaps for data between two dates. You can set up two blank dates in your report (start and finish), so that when you run the report you can insert the required dates at that time. This is known in some reporting suites as Runtime Prompt.

Example:

Leavers report for the month of November

Fields:

Employee No	Employee surname	Gender	Cost centre	FTE

Filter (see below) Status = *Leaver*

Runtime Prompt = Date between 01st November 2017 – 30th November 2017

Filters are used to refine the raw data in your report, for example, a headcount report for the end of November for the office in Manchester

Headcount report as at 30th November

Fields:

Employee No	Employee surname	Gender	Cost centre	FTE

Filters:

Status = *Current*

Date = 30th November 2017

Location = Manchester

Some other examples of the most commonly used reports are:

Salaries:

Employee No	Employee surname	Cost centre	Annual salary

Long Service:

Employee No	Employee surname	Date joined	Years of service

This would be run as at a specific date.

Location

Employee No	Employee surname	Cost centre	Location

Employee Turnover:

No. of employees (within given period) x 100 divided by Average Number of Employees

Stability (example shown for annual figure)

Number of employees with 1 years' service x 100 divided by Number of Employees employed 1 year ago.

Gender Pay Gap reporting

I know many HR people will be thinking about the obligatory reporting on gender pay gap which kicks off in 2017 for organisations with over 250 employees.

The draft regulations require employers to publish:

Employers are required to calculate the percentage difference between the:

- mean (average) gross hourly pay of women in relation to men

- the mid-point (median) gross hourly pay value of women in relation to men.

- The mean and median difference (in percentage terms) between the pay of men and women throughout the organisation.

- The organisation is to be divided into four pay quartiles and the number of men and women in each quartile is to be published.

- The mean (but not the median) percentage difference in bonus paid to men and women.

- The percentages of men and women who receive a bonus.

Employers will not have to publish data by job type or grade, or for full or part-time employees as was originally envisaged. This change was in response to fears that the data would allow individuals to be identified, thus breaching confidentiality.

Bonuses and allowances are included but overtime is not.

Your system's reporting module will help you to do the heavy lifting fairly simply. Here I am showing a fairly basic set up.

Working with the draft guidelines currently available you will need a first cut report something like:

Employee Number	Department	Gender	Salary (p.a.)	Hours (p.w.)	Hours (p.a.)*	Hourly pay
001	Sales	M	25000	35	1820	13.74
002	Accounts	F	17000	35	1820	9.34
003	Accounts	F	18000	35	1820	9.89
004	Marketing	M	24500	35	1820	13.46
005	Marketing	F	19500	30	1560	12.50
006	HR	F	24000	35	1820	13.19
007	IT	M	26000	35	1820	14.29
008	Admin	F	18000	35	1820	9.89
009	Admin	F	17250	35	1820	9.48
010	Assembly	F	9900	20	1040	9.52
011	Assembly	F	9900	20	1040	9.52

- Multiply hours p.w. x 52 in this case

Now re-arrange the report to separate the genders:

002	Accounts	F	17000	35	1820	£9.34
003	Accounts	F	18000	35	1820	£9.89
005	Marketing	F	19500	30	1560	£12.50
006	HR	F	24000	35	1820	£13.19

008	Admin	F	18000	35	1820	£9.89
009	Admin	F	17250	35	1820	£9.48
010	Assembly	F	9900	20	1040	£9.52
011	Assembly	F	9900	20	1040	£9.52
001	Sales	M	25000	35	1820	£13.74
004	Marketing	M	24500	35	1820	£13.46
007	IT	M	26000	35	1820	£14.29

Fig.19 Gender pay gap reporting 1

The total value of hourly pay for women is 83.33

Dividing it by 8 (number of women) gives an average hourly pay figure of **10.42**

The total value of hourly pay for men is 41.49

Dividing it by 3 (number of men) gives an average hourly pay figure of **13.83**

Women's hourly rate is therefore **75.32%** of men's hourly earnings, giving a gap of **24.68%.**

Now sort each gender extract in order of hourly pay:

Female

2	Accounts	F	17000	35	1820	£9.34
9	Admin	F	17250	35	1820	£9.48
10	Assembly	F	9900	20	1040	£9.52
11	Assembly	F	9900	20	1040	£9.52
3	Accounts	F	18000	35	1820	£9.89
8	Admin	F	18000	35	1820	£9.89
5	Marketing	F	19500	30	1560	£12.50
6	HR	F	24000	35	1820	£13.19

Male

4	Marketing	M	24500	35	1820	£13.46
1	Sales	M	25000	35	1820	£13.74
7	IT	M	26000	35	1820	£14.29

Fig.20 Gender pay gap reporting 2

The **median** is the middle value in the list of numbers. Where there is an even set of numbers, the median is arrived at by the average of the two middlemost numbers, i.e. 9.52 and 9.89,(19.41 divided by 2) giving us a median of **9.71**

As there is an odd number of entries for men, the median is easily established as **13.74**

Multiplying 9.71 x 100 and dividing by 13.74, it is shown that women's median hourly rate is **70.67%** of that of men.

Some of these calculations may need to be performed outside of the actual system, but you can see that the raw data can be extracted and then manipulated to facilitate the production of these required figures.

Some reporting suites will also allow you to produce graphic representations such as pie, bar and scatter charts, as well as colour fills and textual explanations, all of which will be familiar to users of Excel.

For those whose managers are unable (or unwilling) to access their reports via the self service system, there is the ability to set up the report to run at scheduled intervals and send via email to specified recipients.

J.   Shift or working patterns

These are usually set up in both HR and Time & Attendance systems, and are key to governing who should be where, and when.

Working patterns for most office staff do not vary.

Examples:

Working pattern number 1: Designated "Standard"

Normal days of work	Monday – Friday inclusive
Hours of work	0900 - 1700
Hours worked (weekly)	35

Employees assigned to this: all apart from exceptions (below)

<u>Working pattern number 2</u>: Designated "Job Share HR Manager 1"

Normal days of work	Monday-Tuesday inclusive	0900 - 1700
	Wednesday	0900 - 1300
Hours worked (weekly)		18

<u>Working pattern number 3</u>: Designated "Job Share HR Manager 2"

Normal days of work	Thursday– Friday inclusive	0900 - 1700
	Wednesday	1400 - 1700
Hours worked (weekly)		17

HR Managers 1 & 2 are then assigned individually to their relevant work pattern.

These are relatively straightforward. The hard work comes in when you are dealing with an environment such as manufacturing or picking & packing, where there are several shifts in a 24-hour day, variable between departments, and changing with the weeks. The combinations can be manifold, and you need to have flexibility to change people or activities between shifts.

Examples:

Assembly division

Designated "**Assembly Shift One**", this shift changes on a three-weekly pattern.

Week One	Monday-Friday	0800-1600
Week Two	Monday-Friday	1600-2400
Week Three	Monday-Friday	2400-0800
Week Four	Monday-Friday	0800-1600

The fourth week reverts back to the pattern as in Week One, and so on.

All employees in this activity will be attached to this shift pattern. To change an employee from this pattern, you merely take them out of this pattern and assign them to another existing one.

Information relating to the above, plus all the rules and processes necessary to inform the configuration operation will be taken back to the vendor so that the software can be set up exactly as the client wants. This is Step 4 in Fig 15.

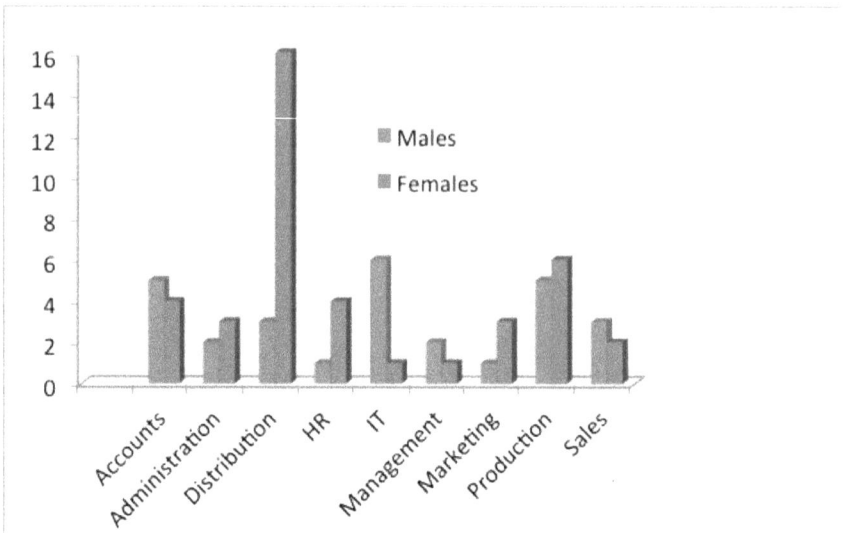

Fig.21 Chart example

It is important to note that the process and authority to modify a shift pattern, or to assign a new shift pattern to an employee must be well-defined in order to avoid conflict with regulations governing employee rights. Nevertheless, where the obtaining of such permission has been complied with, the system changes can be effected easily.

Where an employee fails to clock in at the due time, the system will show them as "non-arrived" until such time as their true status can be confirmed, when the record can be amended manually by the competent person – normally the shift leader or supervisor.

Some time and systems allow working time to to be analysed and reflect across specific activities, either automatically by using different clocking locations or manually where the employee assigns time to a particular costing code. This is valuable at arriving at true costing, particularly in a manufacturing or assembly environment.

Where this feature is required, you will need to tabulate the various activities and codes, and identify the best means by which differentiating between the activities can physically be achieved.

Additionally, time and attendance software can act as an entry system for security access, and here you can configure down to which personnel can access certain parts of the building. For this type of access, I would recommend readers that gather and read biometric data."

K.   Training / Development Administration

The training or development module is a fairly straightforward application that will capture the following:

Course data:

- Date/s

- Time/s

- Topic

- Provider

- Location

- Cost

- Certificate or other recognition

- Attendee/s

- Purpose of training (usually either a need identified by performance management reviews or organisational culture, such as induction.

- Professional programs with examinations are usually reported separately in this module.

Reporting out of this module will show that:

a)   Recent employees who have not been through the induction process which happens every month. To sweep up any who joined in the past 6 months:

Fields

Employee No.	Employee surname	Date of joining

Filters:

Date of joining is between current date and previous date (6 months ago)

Induction completed box = N (or blank)

b) Employees who have had further training or development needs identified in the course of performance reviews have in fact fulfilled that requirement.

c) Reports will also give a summary of training attended during the course of a year or other specified period, and the costs attached to them. This does not, of course, guarantee that the relevant skills were acquired as a result, but does mean that future performance can be monitored to assess modification of behaviour.

L. Work flow

As with reports and automatic triggers, there is a considerable amount of thought that needs to go into the compilation of the work flows that are going to replace the usual signature-gathering fests that surround authorisations of every type of organisational transaction.

By now, your process and procedures maps will have become well-thumbed, and they will form the basis for the design of work flows.

For every transaction, there will be an identifiable chain of document/s, events and initiators / authorisers. These will mirror the maps, which in turn reflect the official policy.

Let's take a look at a sample policy and how it would be configured into a work flow.

To recruit a replacement employee, the hiring manager must raise and complete a requisition form. This form will be completed with the relevant information and passed to the divisional finance head who will confirm that the request is within current year budgetary limits. The document then passes to the recruitment department as a formal request to commence recruitment. A copy of this is returned to the hiring manager.

REQUEST FOR REPLACEMENT HIRE FORM

		STEP 1 **COMPLETE FORM**
DIVISION	OPTICAL	
JOB TITLE	SALES SUPERVISOR	
GRADE	3	
SALARY BAND	24,000-28,000	
FTE	1	
COMMENCING	ASAP	
REASON	Replace J Smith leaving 31.03.201	
SIGNED	A M Gordon (electronic sig)	
JOB TITLE	SALES DIRECTOR	
DATE	27.02.2017	
BUDGETARY DATA APPROVED	S.P. Phillips (electronic sig.)	**STEP 2** **FORWARD FOR APPROVAL**
JOB TITLE	DIVISIONAL AC-COUNTANT	
DATE	28.02.2017	**STEP 3** **VERIFY AND APPROVE**
		STEP 4 **SIGNED FORM:** **COPY TO HIRING MANAGER**
		STEP 5 **COPY TO RECRUITMENT**

Fig.22 Request for replacement hire form

This is a very basic illustration, but serves to show how this can be set up. Part of the requisition form can be auto-populated, keyed by the job title, division and grade, which should provide salary band and FTE.

When the hiring manager has completed the form, it can circulate via the self service system (or intranet if so preferred) for approval, be signed and routed back to the initiating manager, who, in turn, forwards a copy to the recruitment department.

CHAPTER 17

INTERNATIONAL

The international dimension is now at the forefront of HRIS development due to the acceleration of globalisation. Language, currency and terminology are now major considerations, added to which are the differing employment terms and compensation and tax regimes applicable to each geographical unit.

All we have been talking about thus far has been premised on the organisation being based in the same country. Now, with globalisation being very much more commonplace we have to consider operations that are based outside of the country in which the parent or holding company is located.

If your international business language is other than English in some locations then you will have to search for software that offers the language/s that you are looking for. Clearly, this will put limitations on your choices.

Likewise, if you want keep your pay and reward records in local currencies, you will need a system that offers the multicurrency feature. Many international companies will use a standard dollar / euro or sterling conversion for these transactions.

Different countries have different rules, regulations and compliance: statutory holidays, sick pay, standard reporting requirements and so on. On top of that, the syntax used for certain fields will need to change. Accordingly, you will need to separate the database into segments reflecting each operational territory.

Will you use the same range of job titles and departments across the whole spectrum, or will you have a large amount of local autonomy? Where will system administration reside? Some centralised organisations prefer to use a homogenous set of job titles and rank on a global basis so that they can spot or track talent look right across the organisation.

Territory	Country	Language	Currency	System Admin
UK	UK	English	GBP	Yes
Europe	France	English	Euro	UK
	Germany	English	Euro	UK
	Sweden	English	Euro	UK
Asia	India	English	USD	UK
Pacific	Australia	English	USD	UK
	New Zealand	English	USD	UK
N America	USA	English	USD	Yes
	Canada	English	USD	N.Am
LatAm	Mexico	Spanish	USD	Yes
	Costa Rica	Spanish	USD	Mexico
	Colombia	Spanish	USD	Mexico

Fig.23 International Matrix

In fig 23 we can see that the organisation has been divided into six discrete territories, using two languages and three currencies. Segments of the database will be identified by the codes used in the global chart of accounts, such as LatAm being territory code 06 and Mexico 0601, Costa Rica 0602 and so forth. System admin has been devolved to three countries to serve various territories.

For this to work well, there needs to be good communication between the system administrators and a global change control log as a master record of all system admin. transactions.

Where countries need extra or different fields for data, these can be added in; with a little configuration, they will appear as "greyed out" in the profiles of territories where they do not apply.

If your records and currencies are all kept in English, then you can still use a vendor who only sells into the UK market provided that it is hosted in the UK (either by the vendor or by you) and accessible via the internet.

Where your organisation is scattered across the planet, it is important that all personnel accessing and transacting on the system are imbued with the same sense of immediacy, otherwise your reporting is not in real time due to some pile of unprocessed stuff sitting in an in tray somewhere.

Now we come to the intricate part – payroll.

Let us start by saying there is no payroll system on Earth that will handle payments in the near-200 countries of the world; and it won't happen any time soon. Of course, there are systems that have identified generic processes that are performed everywhere and have tailored their offering accordingly, but unless you are a major employer, this probably won't work out as cost-effective.

If you are operating in a handful of what are termed "developed" countries, your chances of finding one payroll supplier for all are reasonable, but, again, the options available may prove to be costly

Our team was called on a couple of years ago by a US client who wanted to have an HR and payroll system that could work for their European subsidiaries in a number of countries. The challenge was to find an HR system that would be the initial entry point both for HR and payroll.

The starting position was this:

- The US parent had HR and payroll systems (not integrated)

- The seven European subsidiaries had no HR system beyond spreadsheets, but each country had their payroll processed by a variety of local means.

- The pay summaries were transmitted back to the US for consolidation into their group ledger.

- HR information was patchy, inaccurate and not up to date.

First, we produced a diagram of the information flows as they stood.

Country	HR	Payroll
US parent	HR software	Payroll software
Euro A	Spreadsheet	Local bureau
Euro B	Spreadsheet	Local bureau
Euro C	Spreadsheet	Manual
Euro D	Spreadsheet	Local bureau
Euro E	Spreadsheet	Local bureau
Euro F	Spreadsheet	Local bureau
UK	Spreadsheet	Payroll software
Financial info back to US ledgers		

Fig.24 Starting point for international solution

After considerable thought we arrived at what we thought was a workable solution to the problem.

We needed:

- A configurable HR system that would provide a user interface for HR and payroll information. The HR data would be logged into the database, and the payroll data would stream through the conduit fields to the payroll providers in each country, all in real time.

- A standard template to be populated by each payroll provider and sent back to the centre at weekly or monthly intervals.

Fig. 25 shows us in simplified terms how this came out.

All HR and payroll information was posted only once through the unified user interface in the HR software solution. Payroll specific information was segregated out and funnelled through the system to the payroll providers by electronic flat file (i.e. a simple file containing just data). They, in turn, processed the payrolls, and then returned the batch payroll information to the US ledgers in a specific format.

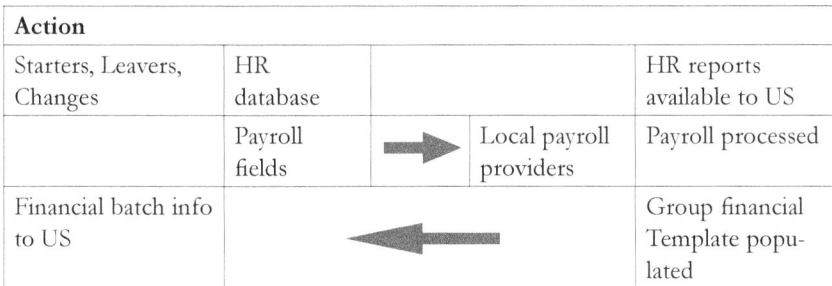

Action			
Starters, Leavers, Changes	HR database		HR reports available to US
	Payroll fields	→ Local payroll providers	Payroll processed
Financial batch info to US		←	Group financial Template populated

Fig.25 International client solution

There are also suppliers who provide a pay aggregator service. In straight-forward terms, this involves the supplier offering a global contract for all the countries involved, and they in turn contract with local providers to receive and / or submit payroll data in a standard format, as well as paying accurately, in timely fashion and in compliance

These suppliers could be your existing ones, or the aggregator may suggest alternatives where the client is not too happy with their payroll supplier's performance.

In this instance, as the client was sourcing new HR software in any case, it was felt that configuration of the HR software to meet the case for the total number of employees involved was a simpler solution than contacting a third party. However, I would say that for larger-scale employee numbers, the pay aggregator model would probably be a more painless solution.

CHAPTER 18

THE NEW SOFTWARE

For everything to work from the first moment you switch on, you need to have worked through all aspects of the system's infrastructure beforehand.

The physical set up of the new software will depend on whether you opted for the vendor to host your new software, or decided to host the application on your own servers.

In the former case, a Test environment will be created at the vendor's base, accessible by browser link. In the latter, your IT /ICT department will allocate a server and loading a copy of the application on to it, ready for data entry.

A further environment will also be set up, the Live Environment, which will be the permanent home for your application when it is tested and ready. It is possible, if required, to ask for a third environment for testing specific untried or speculative operations to see if they really work. (Step 3 in Fig.15)

Once this is set up, the prepared data will be migrated into this environment, and reports run so that they can be checked and validated against the actual existing database. In the case of first time buyers, the reports will need to be compared with whatever form of records are currently kept. (Steps 6 & 7 in Fig.15)

Some standard transactions either from real or fabricated data will be introduced into the test database to see if the desired actions actually take place and give the correct result. These are preliminaries to full parallel running (Steps 8-9 in Fig.15)

- Data Migration (populating the new application)

Step 5 in Fig.15

Many applications are populated by uploading a series of related spreadsheets (usually .csv derived from Excel) by way of a data importer.

Vendors will offer to perform the whole migration for a fee, and this charge can vary enormously

You can get involved in this process by requesting the spreadsheet templates from the vendor, and populate them from your newly-cleansed data sources. You will find that you will need to take your basic data reports – now in spreadsheet form, and make the headings and data formats replicate those of the receiving software, e.g.

Report headings for cells in your system..

Employee No.	Date of birth	Date joined	Department	Job title

..could look like these in the new software:

Emp_no	DOB	DOJ	Dept	Job

Each of these headings must be changed to mirror the new ones, and should be in exactly the same order and formats.

This does not mean that these system headings will be visible to the users; these are only headings used "behind the scenes" in the software. The actual headings will be very much of your choosing during the configuration.

Although this is time-consuming, it is a very good sense check on the data that you have, and gives you at least a bit more ownership and control over it; you will find at times during a project that there are times that it seems like something happening elsewhere!

• History Carried Forward

Ask any project team about history to be brought on to the new system and I can guarantee a variety of responses.

Payroll history is easy to manage, as only the current tax year is held live and previous data is held as an archive. These must be accessible for not less than three years by statute (and I would keep rather more, just in case), so you will need to have arrangements in place for this to comply.

Time and Attendance records, too, are not usually carried forward from previous holiday years. It is advisable to retain a reasonable amount of this data, perhaps 3 years, as it may be relevant to possible disciplinary action, or litigation in respect of Sickness Absence and Industrial injury.

HR records are rather more difficult to decide upon. It's probably fair to say that the longer an employee is with an organisation, the thinner the file! The tendency is to gather more and more information about newer employees, and the trend is escalating.

Factors that should affect the amount of employee history will include:

- How often do you actually refer to records more than a year old?

- Does anyone ever look back at career progression over the past 10 years?

- Just how accurate – and detailed -is the history?

- Training and professional attainments should be included wherever possible.

The more history you bring forward, the more costly it becomes. Every historical post going back in time must be created, populated, and then depopulated as the employee moves on, even though the jobs, and occasionally departments, may have passed out of living memory. You are in fact reconstructing the past, and, as previously mentioned, this history may be inaccurate enough as to be of dubious worth.

An effective way of resolving this would be to agree a point in time, say 2/3 years previous to the current migration time, and import this into the new application.

Earlier data can then be retained in a form of History file. You can either go down the (usually) expensive route of paying your existing provider to access your data through a form of viewer, or simply have some hard copy printouts run, sortable in employee number, social security number, surname and whatever other criterion you want them ranged in.

Whatever you decide, avoid the temptation to import poor quality data into the system in the hopes of cleaning it later; this is never going to happen.

Once all the testing has been carried out to complete satisfaction, the data will be decanted from the migration database into the live one, ready for parallel running

- Parallel running

Steps 12-15 in Fig.15

Parallel running refers to the time period during which the new software is run alongside the old so that comparisons can be drawn between the resulting outcomes.

Whether you are moving from one application to another, or to your first computerised HRIS you will need to parallel run - that is, run it alongside your current arrangement, for a period, mainly for testing purposes to compare and validate output as well as to discover any running problems before going live.

One of the most frequent questions we are asked is "how many parallel runs should we do?"

There are no hard and fast rules about the amount of time that this should entail, but it is important to know that "three month's parallel running" need not refer to three months in actual time. It is equally possible to run the previous two months *a posteriori* as it were, by inputting exactly the same material that went into the old system into the new one, running it, and then comparing the outputs. Any variances can be identified, checked, and followed up to analyse any faults that may have occurred.

It goes without saying that the most "mission critical" application is the payroll, and to a lesser extent, Time & Attendance. Both of these run more in "real time" than HR – although when your system is up and running, HR too should be totally current - and therefore should be prioritised.

In the case of payroll, you may want to be completely satisfied that there will be no errors by running perhaps four months' records before committing to live. Remember however, that every parallel run represents a sizeable duplication of effort, and you will need the resources to be able to accomplish that.

Not only payslips must be compared, but also the weekly or monthly batch totals.

If you are still encountering significant discrepancies after two parallel runs, you must quickly establish where the faults lie and correct them, otherwise your project will come unstuck.

As there is twice the volume of work during a parallel run phase, you will need to accommodate this extra burden. Doubling the hours of your existing people is not going to be popular – even at overtime rates – and can also lead to project fatigue.

I would always advise that any backfilling is done from external sources, meaning that your departmental staff are able to get to grips with the new software at the earliest moment. To be ready for this, they will need to be trained beforehand, and this we will deal with next.

- Training on the software

Training on the new software is very much a case of who, what and when.

We can consider three classes of users who will need to be trained:

System administrators

Designated people, ideally from HR and payroll, who will be responsible for all change control that occurs within the system, that is to say forming, modifying or deleting the following fixed values:

- Configurations such as items in drop down boxes and new screens

- All organisational structure, such as companies, departments and locations;

- Post attributes such as Titles, grades, working patterns; standard hours,

- Security access to the system based on grade or other parameters

- Populating posts with budgeted headcount and FTE

- Appending fixed benefits and other data associated with specific posts or grades of post

HR, payroll and associated users (recruitment, training, etc.)

- Entries into the system for starters, leavers and changes of a transactional nature;

- Compiling system reports

- Configuring triggered (automated) actions

- Configuring work flows

- Payroll inputs and payslip / pay statement production

- All other activities as below, where permitted

All other employees

Self service access for:

- Changing permitted personal data

- Viewing other personal data on a "read only" basis

- Viewing payslips and other pay- and benefit-related data

- Logging holiday and viewing remaining entitlements

- Entering personal sickness

- Viewing permitted organisational data such as departmental or organisational chart

- Running reports within assigned authority levels

- Performance review data, according to authority level

System administrators are your system pioneers – in some organisations they are designated "super users" – and they will take to the system like ducks to water. Although you will need to choose them carefully, very often they choose themselves. They need to trained on the system as soon as the data transfer has been effected and validated.

I should say that once the system is up and running, system administrators will normally be able to integrate this new responsibility with their everyday roles *unless* your employee population is large or the organisation has many centres of operation.

HR & payroll users need to be trained ready to launch the parallel runs and beyond. If you are backfilling posts, make sure those contacted people are keeping the old system in play.

Training for all other employees can be conducted as soon as the system is live and working properly, accessing the self service system, and then how to view and update records. For this large body of people for training it is best to organise them into batches according to their various security access and system availability ratings.

Things to remember about training:

- Don't train people until they are able to immediately use it. Even in a week or two, what was learned can be quickly forgotten.

- Make sure you don't cut corners on training spend; leaving those who have been trained to train others is not a good way to kick off on your new software.

- If you have a large turnover of staff, don't let the system knowledge drift away too; I have seen organisations where the capability of running reports had completely disappeared because new starters in HR and payroll had not been given full training, and were merely given dog-eared notes and some time with someone in the department who *also* had been given the most cursory of system knowledge.

- Contact the system provider for a class for new people, which can act as a refresher for others.

- Training appears to "stick" better when the learning is done in the place where you will be using it. Try to arrange your system training on site rather than in some unknown classroom.

- Arrange for user "handbooks" for each type of user to be available online, in hard copy, or preferably both. Ensure that they are kept current and updated with any useful tips and hints that get discovered as time moves on.

CHAPTER 19

THINGS THAT CAN GO WRONG

Anticipating setbacks and factoring in your likely response to them is part of your plan for success. The HRIS project has its own particular hazards.

In this chapter, I'll be summarising for easy reference the many things that can go wrong and why they happen. They are in no particular order of gravity, but individually or collectively they can cause significant headaches.

1. Not having the big picture.

Software doesn't always give a clue as to its true potential. Take MS Excel; there are half a billion users in the world but the majority in no way exploit its full potential. The reverse is true of HR & payroll software, as people's expectations of its capabilities can be way too high.

We need to have the big picture of what are we trying to achieve by having the software. It won't solve faulty or over-elaborate processes, it doesn't drive change programmes and it can't force managers to sign overtime sheets in time for the pay run, yet these are all aspirations that I have seen in product requirements from clients.

The software will reproduce your processes and run according to your rules in a more efficient way, if the configuration has been correctly specified and implemented. If those processes and rules are ambiguous or not well thought through, then this will be reflected in the way your HR software works.

2. Unrealistic timelines

How long before go live? Well, if you've done all that you should have, modern software is pretty speedy to implement. Don't be pushed into making promises to suit political expediency, however; making rash promises about delivery will not help your cause, and could end up with your software being launched half-cooked instead of fully operational.

Your software supplier will have produced a project plan with a timeline. This will have been compiled based on their experience, and assuming that you have done the necessary preparatory work. Furthermore, they will have allocated time resources for their project manager, beyond which you may find yourself in difficulties, so do try to keep things moving forward on track. Of course, there's always the unexpected, so make sure you're able to make decisions quickly if required.

3. Erroneous or false business case

I've seen business cases built on a lot of airy-fairy assumptions, such as "if we had an absence module, sickness absence would be reduced by 50%" or "new software will make everything run smoother" or even "people will use the new software more than they did with the old one". This all cuts very little ice with the Finance Director who will be looking for Return on Investment. Apart from software nowadays being less costly, you can demonstrate the time savings to be made from your new software and the reduction of errors due to less manual intervention.

As we mentioned in 1, software won't solve your absence problem – your managers do. The system will give them accurate data, and perhaps even trends, but it's the human intervention that will manage the problem.

Remember, too, that once your system is in and running, the very same people to whom you presented the business case will be peering over your shoulder to see if it has been justified!

4. Failure to make the new software a business priority

You got sign-off from the FD, all looked like plain sailing…and then the project was put on "the back burner" due to some corporate logjam devouring resources. Put simply, you didn't put enough emphasis on how important the new software was to the organisation; it's all there in the business case.

Make sure you get commitment as well as a signature.

5. Not enough resource – money and manpower availability committed to the project

For the whole project to work, it needs to be properly resourced. Once the green light has been given, there is a massive amount of preparatory work to be undertaken, and this means extra people to backfill. Again, the implementation phase where two systems are being operated during testing and parallel running will require additional temporary headcount. And then there's the question of your own project manager .

6. Failure to illustrate the benefits throughout the organisation and secure support.

The benefits you illustrate in your business case will need to be presented in a different light to users and internal 'clients'. They won't be interested in the fact that the new system saves forty seconds per transaction due to enhanced speed and fewer screens, or that self service and work flow enables overtime and expenses payments to be brought to process much faster. They'll want to see if it's intuitive, can be personalised and what's in it for them, like improved reporting.

Don't underestimate the amount of communication you'll need to ensure a smooth change in culture. If you are bringing in self service or electronic payslips, you'll need careful managing and skilful presentation to the wider audience to gain acceptance.

Bear in mind too, that actions that can bring about a culture change – especially things like e-payslips and self service – need careful managing and skilful presentation to the wider audience.

7. Weak project sponsor

Your project sponsor is a key player in this exercise. They need to be fully behind the project, and to lend heavyweight support to ensure that the right amount of resource is made available as and when required. If they are not prepared to stand up and be counted when the going gets tricky – and it will – then the chances of a successful outcome are going to be much reduced. Choose wisely (see #9)

7. Not getting the right people on board

I am certainly no fan of organisational politics, but one has to be aware of certain people whose support is crucial. They may actually be only on the periphery of the scope of your project – or perhaps not affected by it at all – but they need to be brought 'into the loop' and kept there.

It seems incredible, but it's very true; I saw one project stopped dead in its tracks because some political heavyweight hadn't been consulted. This is where your savvy project sponsor can help to smooth the way ahead.

8. Insufficient preparation

This has to be up there with the major reasons for failure of your software project. By preparation, I'm talking about mapping your key processes (e.g. Starters, Leavers, Changes, Recruitment , Absence and Performance management), assembling all the organisational Rules (such as Pay frequencies, Overtime rates, Holiday entitlements, Benefits, Working hours, Maternity/Paternity pay and Occupational sick pay) as opposed to the statutory ones that will already be in the software.

Added to this, you'll need to have diagrams of the structures of your organisation to reflect departmental or divisional set-up, the hierarchy of jobs within those structures with reporting lines, together with grades and any dependent benefits.

It's a big job; in my experience, all this information is scattered around; some in HR, some in payroll, the employee handbook and so on. It needs to be gathered in one place for this project.

You'll see the importance of this when we say that this information

a) Provides a good guide to what your system should comprise;

b) Informs you and your prospective vendor of how the software needs to be configured

c) Enables you to build scenarios for product demonstrations.

d) Is the blueprint for your project manager and the vendor's counterpart to drive implementation?

If you don't do any or all of this you are heading for major problems later, and if you think you can short circuit all this hard work by blithely asking for recommendations from your LinkedIn network – forget it. Their experience is unique, could have required different desired outcomes to yours and may not be objective

9. Failure to thoroughly cleanse data before importing.

In the past, some clients have proposed that they would import the data "as is" -even though it is known to be dodgy - and correct it later. The idea was that some poor soul would go through the whole database and make the necessary amendments over time.

That, of course, would never happen, and the first inaccurate reports from your new system will scupper all your credibility.

It's not too difficult to do an updated data request from your employees in advance of the data importation and make sure all is pristine when it appears in your new software

10. Not researching enough choice

You need to give yourself every chance of success, and making sure you cover all the possibilities is essential. For that reason, don't confine your research to the big names (which could be too large or costly for what you really need).

Go to the big exhibitions such as CIPD's HR software show in June each year; check out sites like HRcomparison, and do online research. It's a combination of these three that will give you the widest net.

From this wide trawl you can filter down to your long list, and when you have more detail from vendors get to your target short list for product demonstrations.

11. Too concerned with budget

Organisations nearly always tend to try to go for the cheapest option. If it turns out the best fit has the lowest price, great, but it is not always going to be the case.

I've always found the best outcomes have come from the approach of 'let's find what's right' rather than 'how much can we get away with'.

Unless you are going in for the massive ERP systems, modern software is quite affordable now, and there are easier ways of paying. The days of having to ante up a huge initial payment are well past.

The demonstration has historically turned out to be a 'killing field' for the ambitions of HR and payroll practitioners. In order to maximise our chances we need to have done all the earlier work.

12. Poorly structured demonstrations

In terms of failure this is probably the Daddy of them all, mainly due to so much of the selection process being influenced by them.

What typically has happened before is that the vendor is invited to spend time showing the potential client 'what the system can do', showing how it handles absence, sets up diaries, runs off dazzling reports and a host of other, very useful features. Enough to make anyone want to pull out a pen and sign up.

What is not happening, of course, is seeing how the product can work in the specific way that the client needs. The presence of a module such as Absence does not mean that it can be configured to work in the way you need it to.

To do this, you need to compile sample scenarios (worked up using your previously prepared process maps and rules) and let the vendor have these beforehand so that they can see if they can comply. This also includes reports; those dazzling showpieces may actually need a Doctorate in Logic to prepare when you see them put together step-by-step.

Backing all this up, you need to have scoresheets, so that you allocate points for each question and how it is covered.

The key to all this is that **you drive the agenda for the demonstration**, and it should be tightly scripted to maximise the use of time. Don't allow things to wander into areas which may be really 'sexy' but of no use to you.

13. Not engaging professional project manager

The temptation for any HR or payroll manager is to personally take charge of managing the client side of the implementation cycle, or even appoint someone from their team to do it. Don't even go there, unless they are experienced project people who can effectively marshal the resources and the time constraints, manage the liaison with the vendor's PM, and communicate clearly with the steering team or sponsor.

Because the project can throw up the unexpected, it's not an activity than can be undertaken in addition to the day job, so you'll need to back fill, in which case, why not bite the bullet and get a professional?

Of course, it's a cost, but this should have been budgeted in your business case, and as the project is business critical, there's nothing to be achieved by trying to trim unnecessarily. This project is important to the organisation, the department – and you! Don't ruin its chances by turning it into 'amateur night.'

14. Changing requirements while the project in progress aka 'Mission Creep'

There sometimes comes a moment when someone has a Bright Idea. "Why don't we….?" It takes root somehow, and before you know it, the project has an additional series of problems to overcome, and some new cost implications.

An example: Part way through implementation one client wanted to give their HR system the additional functionality of a data warehousing system, something that the selected software was not designed to do. After some study, fortunately, the client was persuaded that the costs accruing from this were not supported by the eventual benefits, and after a spell of indecision the idea was squashed.

If the right thinking processes have been done beforehand, this sort of distraction shouldn't happen, but, be on your guard.

15. Failure to train sufficiently

I've seen plenty of cases where, both to cut costs and due to work pressure, system training was reduced to a minimum. This is a serious mistake. Users need to be proficient and comfortable with using the software.

Avoid the work load issues by ensuring you have backfill resources to relieve pressure on your regular team.

It doesn't stop there, by the way. Long after your system is in and running, make sure that all new users of the system are given proper training in it. A sketchy half hour sitting with an overworked current user just doesn't cut it; I can cite the case of one client where due to this very issue, the department had lost the capability to produce its own reports, and had to ask the IT department for assistance each time.

Conclusion

The failures we have look at here should serve as a 'heads up' rather than a deterrent. You minimise the risk of failure by investing work, resource and patience into your project and the reward is knowing that you organisation will benefit as a result.

CHAPTER 20

ENDGAME

Your journey has begun, but although your whole focus is now on the new software, don't forget your old data, and how you may need to access it.

After the successful launch of the project, you should consider it as a permanent "work in progress" to continue developing and improving HR- & payroll-related processes, and the quality of information available to all levels of the organisation.

Even as your organisation is successfully getting to grips with their new software, there are still a number of items left on your list to be dealt with.

The first thing, if it hasn't already been done, is to serve notice on your current supplier and start to negotiate the way out. I referred to this at the very end of chapter four.

You will need to agree that existing systems should be maintained until complete cut-over to the new application is complete, at which point they can be decommissioned by being cleared down and withdrawn from the operating platform.

Ensure that all master copies are accounted for are returned to the original vendor, or disposed of in line with their wishes.

Modern browser-enabled systems are easier to shut off, which leaves the rather more complicated issue of historical data that is currently held on the system.

Payroll is required to be accessible for a recommended period of five years, and HR is an ongoing record. The main options are:

- Maintaining an environment version of the previous application, where records can be accessed and read via a viewer version of your previous software.

- Data converted into a contemporary format such as Excel where it can be used at will;

- The old-fashioned giant pile of printout.

The first two have a cost attached; a) is usually an ongoing rental charge and b) is a one-time charge. Neither is particularly cheap and quotations can vary wildly.

The last option is not as impractical as it might sound; people generally over-estimate the amount of access they need to historical data over time. Providing the history reports are produced in a range of sorts (Surname, Employee Number, National Insurance Number, Operating Division) then look-ups are not time-consuming.

The point about having a good system is that you can develop it as you become more familiar with it. Some vendors will have a client account representative assigned to you, so use them as a bridge for suggestions to be fed back to the "laboratory" when the software engineers are.

You will also need to be aware of the culture change issues as you unroll more initiatives, particularly in the area of self service which will impact all your employee base. As you develop the functionality, make sure it is thoroughly tested first before releasing on the organisation. Above all, make sure your data accuracy is maintained *at all times*. People will be responsible for their own personal data, true, but it will be the data that appears at corporate level which will be your responsibility. Bear this in mind at all times.

As we have said before, there is probably no 'perfect fit' for you; as with most things in life, there is always a compromise, unless you are prepared to spend a lot of money customising the product. Customisation can, in many cases, indicate that a particular existing process is being replicated on the new technology. I would reiterate the advice to look again at all your processes, work flows and procedures, to weed out inefficiency and introduce improvements, before bringing them on to the new software.

Vendors have come a long way in the last 10 years; the hard sell and worry about the rest "in the next release" later has gone, and in its place is a more sustainable model. With good reason; who wants a client continuously complaining for several years?

In the future, vendors will also need to take responsibility for their on-site consultants understanding client issues, and not instituting "quick fixes" because of project pressures with other clients.

Let all remember that client and vendor are working together and to the same end; it's just that in future it won't be for quite such a long period of time.

It is correspondingly incumbent upon potential clients to make themselves more informed; if you start your conversation with a vendor with "so what does your software do?" then you only have yourself to blame.

I would like to say a few words about the UK institutions (the Chartered Institute for Personnel and Development (*CIPD*) and the Chartered Institute of Payroll Professionals (*CIPP*) and their responsibility for educating their students, the future HR and payroll heads of the future.

In my opinion, there is still a way to go in the way these students are familiarised with HRIS, both in the business strategy side and with the practical planning and execution of an HRIS project. The increased focus on analytics coming out of HRIS must surely accelerate this need, and I look forward to these leading bodies upping their game to take account of this.

And so, there you have it. I started off compiling this book some time ago, not only with the intention of casting some light on what, prima facie was a very arcane topic with a high casualty rate, but also to give HR and payroll professionals the courage and confidence to embar on the project with a better degree of certainty of a winning result.

I hope that I have gone some way to achieving this, and to every reader, may I wish you every success in your endeavours.

GLOSSARY

(reproduced by kind permission of HRcomparison Ltd)

Absence Module

The part of the HRIS that collects and aggregates information on attendance, holidays and sickness.

The module can be populated by direct input from paper records, via an employee self service portal or by upload from a data importer or time & attendance application.

Some absence modules facilitate use of the Bradford Factor *(q.v.)* method of evaluating sickness absence.

Appeals (see Employee Relations)

Applicant Tracking System – ATS *(see e-recruitment)*

Artificial Intelligence

The development and execution of computer applications and systems that are intended to carry out tasks that hitherto needed human intervention or intelligence, such as visual and speech recognition, translation of languages, compiling and running reports, and processes leading to actual making of decisions based on data available to it.

Audit Trail

This is normally accessed through the system admin. area and will detail every transaction through the application, date and by whom generated.

Regular checks of this are essential to verify the integrity of the data, and to trace the origin of errors emanating from the system.

Auto Number Generation

This is the function where, once set up (usually in system admin.) unique employee numbers are generated as soon as a new employee is entered onto the application.

On configuring the system, existing sequences are loaded in via data importer. In some cases, existing organisational sequences cannot be accommodated by the software. It is important for employees to have only one number, irrespective of the number of posts or roles they may hold, particularly if they appear on the payroll.

Automated Events (*see Triggered Events*)

Big Data

Big Data can be defined as a data mass consisting of structured (and unstructured) data elements that are difficult to process using conventional database methodology. It is a challenge to collate as data is captured by a range of devices of varying sophistication, e.g. video cameras, supermarket terminals, loyalty cards, transport tickets, official records, phone records and press cuttings, etc.

This data is of interest as it can be mined or analysed for the extraction of trends and patterns of behaviour such as travel patterns, buying preferences, and personal tendencies in certain situations.

The term "Big" is relative, and what is considered "Big" today, could be pretty Average tomorrow.

Information contained on HRIS can be considered as a part of Big Data, but it is subject to considerable data protection.

Bradford Factor

The Bradford factor is a way of illustrating how disruptive frequent short-term absence – around weekends for example – can be, relative to occasional longer spells of absence. Bradford scores are a way of identifying individuals with serious absence and patterns of absence worthy of further investigation. It helps highlight causes for concern and often is one of the first steps in an attendance procedure. (IDS definition)

The Bradford Factor score is calculated as S x S x D

S=the number of absences in the last 52 weeks

D=total number of days' absence during the same period.

Example:

Calculation

	S x S x D	Score
One absence of 7 days	1 x 1 x 7	7
Two absences of 2 days & one of 3 days	3 x 3 x 7	63
Seven absences of 1 day each	7 x 7 x 7	343

Fig.26 Bradford Factor example

The higher the score, the greater the disruption.

This can of course be reflected over varying rolling periods of time.

Some HR software includes Bradford Factor statistics already built into the absence module..

Business Intelligence Application

A piece of software that enables the user to report, analyse and present data that is held either in other modules of the same system, or in other discrete systems. The software typically straddles other applications e.g. HR software, payroll software, time & attendance or finance systems and is set up to draw data from them.

Catalogue

The catalogue within an HRIS is the array of fields used in the database application that are reflected in the report writer, e.g. Job Title, Surname, Grade and Salary.

It is essential that every new field that is added by the user organisation (via the system administration module for change control consistency) is *automat-*

ically updated to the catalogue, otherwise it cannot appear in the reports.

The places in HR software where the database meets the report writer are commonly known as "joins". Up to a few years ago, it wasn't unusual for software to be supplied with some joins incomplete, that caused a lot of head-scratching in HR departments trying out their new-found report writing skills, but fortunately most HRIS will automatically update their catalogues with new fields.

Chatbot

Normally encountered online, a chatbot is a tool that has been designed to simulate interaction with humans, and will typically form the first line of contact on entry to a website or computer program."

Cloud Computing

Cloud computing is a model for enabling convenient, on-demand network access to a shared pool of configurable computing resources (e.g., networks, servers, storage, applications, and services) that can be rapidly configured and released with minimal intervention from either party. This reduces the costs to individuals and organisations alike.

The principle is that any computer connected to the internet is connected to a common pool resource, in terms of computing power and software options. The cloud model promotes availability and features five main characteristics:

- On-demand self-service

- Broad network access

- Pooling of resource

- Fast flexibility to expand or contract

- A measurable service

Comma Separated Values

Generally referred to as a .csv file, this is used, amongst other things, to transfer data between applications. Typically used when importing / exporting data between old and new HR & payroll systems or bulk uploading data such as Absence records via a data importer.

Configuration

There is often confusion in client's minds about the difference between configuration and customisation, particularly when sourcing HR software.

Configuration is basically the setting up, addition, modification or deletion of parameters and rules within the application, such as Holiday Entitlements, Occupational Sick Pay limits, Posts and Benefits. The ability to do this is inherent in the system. Consultancy assistance is usually employed at the roll out of an application, and thereafter is performed by system administrators within the user department.

Customisation

Is modification of the original software, in order to accommodate a client's requirements, such as new screens and new categories. This entails radical changes, and can be costly. It is often advisable to look into what is driving the need for customisation, as it may be that a straightforward replication of existing processes can be re-worked to advantage.

Customisation can also cause difficulties when the product is updated or upgraded.

(See also: Configuration above)

Data Importer

A Data Importer is a software feature that runs a routine to move data from one application to another. For example, data is drawn from one source, perhaps in Excel format, is converted into another format (e.g. csv, comma separated values file) and then drawn into another application in order to to populate it.

Most new or upgraded HRIS are populated by this method as it saves keying in all the data again. The most common way for a new system to be populated is by importing a number of related spreadsheets set out in a specific format.

This emphasises the need to ensure that all data is clean before migrating it to another application.

Disciplinary (see Employee Relations)

Email Client

E-mail software, such as Microsoft Outlook Express or Lotus Notes.

Also called a mail client (or just client), is software that enables you to send, receive, and organise email.

Employee Relations

Employee Relations is the generic term for the part of the HR software that covers Discipline, Grievance and Appeal. The stages of these processes are tracked through the application, and will generate reminders where required. Not the least important of these reminders is the one that can be set up to purge warnings from the system in line with organisational policy.

Employee Self Service (ESS)

ESS is a web based application that provides employees with a portal to access their personal records (address, contact, and emergency contact details) and their payroll records (bank account and payslips).

Employees to have the facility to change or modify certain fields such as address, bank details or emergency contact, as well as generate requests for holidays, training or report on sickness absence.

More advanced iterations of ESS feature the capability of running appraisal reporting online and connecting it to objective setting and training / developmental needs, which in turn can be administratively booked and delivered through the ESS application.

Layers of security within the ESS application can permit managers to view records and requests relating to their staff or departments.

ESS can operate as a feature on an organisation's intranet or via a web enabled proprietary self service module appended to an HR system. Logically, it is most effective when deployed across a mainly PC user population.

Entry System

Not to be confused with a time & attendance system, this is a system that permits entry by use of an identification tag. Some entry systems will collect basic data as to the ID and timings of people effecting entry. There are some time & attendance applications that enable entry as part of their capabilities.

e-learning (see learning management system (LMS))

Equal Opportunities Monitoring

Note: the categories listed are those commonly used within the UK context for Equal Opportunities Monitoring. You can choose to vary these as monitoring is a configurable feature on HRIS.

Gender

Date of Birth

Ethnic Group

- White – British
- White – Irish
- White Scottish
- Irish Traveller
- Other White background
- Black or Black British – Caribbean
- Black or Black British – African
- Other Black background
- Asian or Asian British – Indian
- Asian or Asian British – Pakistani
- Asian or Asian British – Bangladeshi
- Chinese
- Other Asian background
- Mixed – White & Black Caribbean
- Mixed – White & Black African
- Mixed – White & Asian
- Other Mixed background
- Other ethnic background
- Not known
- Do not wish to supply

Religion or Belief

- Christian
- Buddhist
- Hindu
- Jewish
- Muslim

- Sikh
- None
- Prefer not to say
- Other – please specify:

Marital Status

- Single
- Married
- Prefer not to Say

Sexual Orientation

- Bi-sexual
- Heterosexual
- Gay
- Lesbian
- Other
- Prefer not to say

Disability or Long-Term Illness

- No known disability
- Dyslexia
- Blind/partially sighted
- Deaf/have a hearing impairment
- Wheelchair user/have mobility difficulties
- Personal care support
- Mental health difficulties
- An unseen disability, eg diabetes, epilepsy, asthma
- Multiple disabilities
- A disability not listed above
- Not known
- Prefer not to say

e-recruitment (also known as Applicant Tracking System – ATS)

e-recruitment (or online recruitment) is part of the talent management process, using web technology to attract, recruit and process employees through organisational systems. Applicants are able to apply for positions posted on the organisation's website or job board, and those applications are filtered and then streamed directly to the hiring manager.

ERP

ERP stands for Enterprise Resource Planning, typically a software application or combination of applications that manages and coordinates information and resources within an organisation. HRIS (Human Resources Information Systems) will form part of an ERP application.

Escrow

Software or source code escrow is a form of insurance to cover the contingency of your HR software supplier going out of business.

Under the terms, a copy of the source code (which is the programme written by the developer) is lodged with an agreed third party, an escrow agent, who would release the code to you under specifically agreed conditions, enabling you to recruit assistance to keep the programmes running.

There is a cost attached to this, and in most cases purchasers will have satisfied themselves as to the good standing of their chosen vendor. However, due diligence requirements in some sectors tend to the heavily risk-averse, and this is the solution for them.

FTE (Full Time Equivalent)

The basis on which Headcount is calculated, 1.0 FTE is represented by a full-time employee working standard organisation hours.

If a standard full-time employee works 40 hours per week, an employee working 25 hours per week is expressed as 0.63 FTE. On most systems, you can set up each post with its budgeted FTE, and compare the budgeted FTE to the actual people in post, and highlight the differences (usually expressed as vacancies).

Fat Client

A fat client or rich client is computer architecture which typically provides considerable functionality independently of the central server. Originally known as just a 'client' or 'thick client', the name is derived as an opposite to "thin client", describing a computer which heavily depends on a server's applications.

A fat client still requires at least periodic connection to a network or central server, but is often characterised by the ability to perform many functions without that connection. In contrast, a thin client generally does as little processing as possible and relies on accessing the server each time input data needs to be processed or validated.

Grievance (see Employee Relations)

Grossed Up Pay

From time to time, employers want to ensure that an employee receives a particular net amount of money, in which case a reverse calculation must be performed to arrive at the gross figure before deductions such as PAYE and National Insurance.

Some payroll providers will enable this computation as a standard feature, which cuts out the arduous manual method.

Hay Job Evaluation

Hay Job Evaluation is one of the most popular business management methodologies devised for the analysis of all the existing roles within an organisation. It can be used to produce an organisation chart enabling the grading and banding of salaries and benefits and ranks jobs at similar or varying levels of responsibility.

http://www.haygroup.com/ww/services/index.aspx?ID=111

Hosted service

Rather than be downloaded, the software is provided by a hosted service provider and is generally paid for on a monthly/annual basis; also known as the application service provider (ASP) software model. Some of these services also charge a percentage of sales in addition to the monthly fee.

This model often has predefined templates that a user can choose from to customize their look and feel. In this model users typically have less ability to modify or customize the software with the advantage of having the vendor continuously keep the software up to date for security patches as well as adding new features added.

HRIS

HRIS stands for Human Resources Information System (or Human Resource Information Software) and is a generic term for software elements dealing with the recording and processing of personnel.

Other commonly used terms are HRMS (Human Resource Management System or Human Resource Management Information System) and Human Capital Solutions,

HRIS software can form part of a suite in larger organisations.

These applications are commonly referred to as Enterprise Resource Planning applications (**ERP q.v.**)

Integrated Applications

In an HRIS context, these applications share a common database although may perform differing functions, e.g. HR & payroll or payroll and time & attendance.

Interface

In HRIS, a user interface is the part of a program that connects the computer with the user and there are interfaces to connect programs, to connect devices, and to connect programs to devices.

The main feature of interfaces is to connect seamlessly between two applications, and they can be costly to construct. Some HR & payroll packages are actually two different applications with an interface facilitating their working together (as opposed to integrated applications that share a common database)

They are not to be confused with data importing / exporting, where there is a distinct input or output from one application, which needs to be imported into or exported from another.

Invitation to Tender (ITT) – (see Tendering - various terminologies)

Learning Management System (LMS)

This is a more advanced application than the conventional training administration module. Typically run in conjunction with an employee self service system, an LMS will allow interaction between employee, manager and training provider.

A comprehensive LMS will pick up training and developmental needs from an employee appraisal (either from within the application or from a connected program) and track the whole process from selection of provider, to delivery and beyond.

With LMS, there is also more scope to record the various strands within learning & development, as they can range from induction, compliance renewals (e.g. first aider certificate), NVQs, and professional curricula all the way down to mentoring or observation.

Licensed software

Software is downloaded and then installed on a Web server. There is usually a one-time fee for this, although there are many free products available as well.

The main advantages of this option are that the client owns a license and therefore can host it on any web server that meets the server requirements, and that the source code can often be accessed and edited to customise the application.

Managed Service

A managed service will involve the management – or part management - of the organisational HR or payroll process. It is more common for payrolls to be provided as a managed service than HR.

Vendors will typically provide access to the client on a real-time online basis. For example, data may be input at a client's premises, but the payroll could be run and processed by the vendor.

The amount of management required is usually very flexible, with the client determining the level of involvement by the vendor with their processes.

Offshoring

Offshoring is a type of outsourcing which involves having particular business functions performed in another country. The best-known form of offshoring is to have software code and development done in countries where the cost base is much lower. Payroll, in particular, has experienced an upsurge in offshoring, with processing centres based in Eastern Europe.

Organisation Charts

These charts are derived from the hierarchy on the database, and are a graphical representation of the organisational structure.

Most modern systems now feature their own organisation charting application, but it is not unknown for third party applications (such as OrgPlus and MS Visio) to be bolted inside other systems.

Modern organisations do not conform to the traditional pyramid structure, and are complicated by matrix reporting lines and multi-posts; there are occasions when the application has to be manually overridden on the chart itself to reflect a particularly complex arrangement.

Outsourced Service

Outsourcing involves the transfer of the management and/or day-to-day execution of a business function such as payroll or human resources to an external service provider.

The client and the provider enter into a contractual agreement that defines the transferred services. Under the agreement the supplier acquires the means of production in the form of a transfer of people, assets and other resources from the client. The client agrees to procure the services from the supplier for the term of the contract.

P11D

The P11D is a statutory form required by the tax authority (HMRC) from UK based employers detailing the cash equivalents of benefits and expenses that they have provided during the tax year to their directors, and employees earning at the rate of more than (currently) £8,500 per year.

(source: www.p11dorganiser.co.uk)

Platform

The hardware, operating system and database management or file system.

It may also refer to a specific combination of hardware and operating system

Pre-qualification Questionnaire (PQQ) – (*see Tendering - various terminologies*)

Request for Information (RFI) – (see Tendering -various terminologies)

Request for Proposal (RFP) – (see Tendering - various terminologies)

Self service *(see Employee Self Service)*

Software as a Service (SaaS)

Software as a Service is used to describe the supply of software as a variable overhead rather than a fixed cost. In a sense, it is a new iteration of the "bureau" approach, but instead of a third party providing the processing as well as a software environment it is now supplied more flexibly.

Organisations can plug in and subscribe to services built on world-class infrastructure via the Internet. All they need is a basic computer with an internet browser and an internet connection.

SaaS also changes the traditional model of user licensing as on-demand licensing enables software to become a variable expense, rather than a fixed cost at the time of purchase. It also enables licensing only the amount of software needed versus traditional licenses per device.

Another upside to SaaS is that it can reduce the up-front expense of software purchases, and may lead eventually to a reduction of investment in server hardware as these costs and functions are shifted to the service provider.

Shared Service

Shared Service is the centralisation of a service that had previously existed in more than one part of an organisation, or, indeed, in more than one organisation.

For example, there has been considerable study made in the public sector (local authorities in particular) to amalgamate some of the generic activities such as HR and payroll to provide more flexibility at a notionally reduced cost. Larger organisations also deploy this model, not only on cost grounds but also for consistency of service.

Software Licence

The type of Licence that is most usually encountered in HRIS is a proprietary licence, meaning that the software vendor gives a licence to use an agreed number of copies of the application, but ownership will always reside with the vendor.

There are a number of subsidiary legal issues attaching to software licences that are not to be gone into here; a well-known example of proprietarily licensed software is Microsoft Windows.

A number of HRIS vendors use a charging model based on the number of user licences.

System Administration

The System Administration module is the part of the application where authorised persons are able to configure rules (such as holiday and occupational sickness), add / delete new Posts or modify existing ones (such as amending the FTE), Departments and Divisions and add system users with their appropriate Security access levels.

Additionally to this, the system events (or triggered actions) and work flow functions can be formatted and set in motion from here, where available to the application.

System Events – (*see Triggered Events*)

Talent Management

Talent management is a generic name given to the process of recruiting, managing, improving, evaluating and developing the employee base of an organisation.

It is the end-to-end process of planning, recruiting, developing, managing, and compensating employees throughout the organization.

Talent management software solutions aim to collect elements of what were hitherto disparate activities (recruitment, performance appraisal and development) and relate them back to organisational objectives.

Talent management can be handled by any of the following:

a) using a dedicated Talent management module in an integrated HR product

b) using a stand-alone module in association with an integrated product

c) combining existing fields to create Talent management reports

Tendering – various terminologies

A request for information (RFI) is a standard process used to gather information about the capability or suitability of a series of vendors to supply, in this case HR & payroll software, time & attendance software or other HRIS.

An RFI will follow a standard format, to enable easy comparison and assist the process of selecting a list of vendors who will then be invited to tender by means of a request for proposal (RFP), invitation to tender (ITT), request for tender (RFT) or request for quotation (RFQ).

An RFI can also be known as a pre-qualification questionnaire (PQQ). Typical information required would be financial statements, health & safety policies, equality policies and commentary on the resources available to service the prospective client.

Thin Client

A thin client (sometimes also called a lean or slim client) is a computer network which depends primarily on the central server for processing activities, and mainly focuses on conveying input and output between the user and the remote server. (Contrasting with **Fat Client** q.v. which does as much processing as possible and passes only data for communications and storage to the server)

Many thin client devices run or support web browsers meaning that all major processing is performed on the server.

Time & attendance system

These systems are primarily deployed in production or manufacturing locations, and record employee attendance by "clocking" them in and out by a variety of means

It is possible to allocate employees to a set of shift patterns and plan required workforce patterns. These applications provide powerful reporting tools for a range of production statistics.

It is worth bearing in mind that a substantial hardware cost can be incurred per clocking point, and so their deployment should be carefully considered.

Triggered Actions

Also known as system events, triggered events or automated events, these are features of most HRIS whereby actions are triggered by changes in specified data fields. These responses can take the form of email or SMS alerts.

An example would be when a new employee is entered on the HR database prior to start date the configured triggered action would generate a series of emails to:

- Advise Security & Switchboard of the arriving newcomer, name, position and department;

- Advise the IT department to create an ID and login;

- Advise the relevant departments to provide a car, mobile phone, laptop, where appropriate;

- Advise the Training co-ordinator to enter the new starter on the next Induction programme.

Triggered actions can be setup in the system admin part of the application or by users. They constitute one of the big advantages of HR systems, as they streamline administration and help to suppress errors and oversights.

Upgrade

Upgrade is a term referring to the replacement of a product with a newer version of that same product, typically a replacement of hardware or software to update the system (e.g. annual changes to payroll) or to improve its features or operating efficiency.

Increasingly, the downloading of upgrades is effected via the internet where a "patch"- containing the parts of the application that will be changed – is introduced into the main application.

Web Browser

A software application used to access information from the internet, such as: Internet Explorer or Google Chrome.

Web-Enabled

Able to connect to or run on the web.

Workflow

The automation of a business process, in whole or part, during which documents, information or tasks are passed from one participant to another for action, according to a set of procedural rules. Workflows can be set up either in system admin or by users.

APPENDICES

- Appendix One: Hybrid Tender Document

- Appendix Two: Process Map (Leaver)

- Appendix Three: Supplier demonstrations – Sample scenarios

- Appendix Four: The Big Five Benefits of an HR System

APPENDIX ONE

Below is an example of a hybrid tender document that was produced in conjunction with a client. Some redaction has been done to eliminate client-specific references.

This should provide a very comprehensive template from which you can draw up your own model.

Invitation to Tender – HR & payroll system

CONTENTS

1 Introduction

2 Project

2.1 Scope of Project

2.2 Project Goals and Objectives

3 Background

  3.1 Technical Environment

4 General Requirements

  4.1 The Provider

  4.2 The System

  4.3 User Interface

5 Detailed Functional Requirements

  5.1 Human Resources

  5.2 Payroll

5.3 Security & Audit

6 Supplier Information Required

6.1 General Information

6.2 Application Features

6.3 Technical Specification

6.4 Cost

6.5 Implementation

6.6 Evidence of Capacity to Deliver Contract Requirements

6.7 Data Return

6.8 Terms & Conditions

6.9 Service Level Agreement

7. Management of the Tender Process

7.1 Delivery of Tender

7.2 Opening of Tender

7.3 Timescales

7.4 Queries

7.5 Appendices

7.6 Selection Criteria

INTRODUCTION

Description of Client to reflect:

Population of area served

Functions of Client

Number of people employed (-), working arrangements profile and pay patterns used (paid monthly)

Challenges faced, and rationale for selecting new system.

PROJECT

2.1 Scope of Project

Client is intending to replace its current discrete HR and Payroll systems with a fully integrated HR & Payroll application, to enable the Client to both allow the HR and Payroll departments to work more efficiently and enable the Client to optimise its resources and capacity to support the Service units.

It is intended that this replacement will be effected using as much current technical infrastructure as is possible without any adverse impact on performance.

2.2 Project Goals and Objectives

These include:

An implementation that transitions seamlessly from the current HR and Payroll to the new system

Efficiency through single entry, self-service and automation of process

Higher quality information available to management.

Improved service delivery

Suppression of error risk by reduction of manual intervention

Routine upgrade and maintenance of the application on a planned basis.

BACKGROUND

3.1 Technical Environment

Client's current technical environment is as follows:

3.1.1 Servers

3.1.2 Clients

3.1.3 Internet

3.1.4 Current Business Systems

Client currently uses X HR System and Y payroll system. There is no linkage between the two.

GENERAL REQUIREMENTS

4.1 The Provider:

The provider will be and an established, financially stable Payroll & HR supplier with a proven track-record of delivering both software and outsourced services to the Client market and who is committed to the longer-term support of their product.

The System:

The system should support the functions of: Personnel Management, Recruitment, Training and Payroll.

The provider will be operating software that has full and current HMRC approval.

The system should be upgraded as and when statutory legislation changes, including annual HM Revenue & Customs (HMRC) updates.

The new system should cater for replacing current manual forms and allow managers to input/retrieve the same information and set up the appropriate workflow for authorisation

4.3 User Interface:

A common look and feel across modules which promotes user friendliness

User defined screens enabling access to all required information, with ability to "drill down" to more detailed information

- Data entry validation to force compliance with standards will assist with performance measurement

- Diary/note pad facility across all modules

- Context sensitive on-line help facilities

- Populate standard letters using functions such as Mail Merge.

1. DETAILED FUNCTIONAL REQUIREMENTS

5.1 HUMAN RESOURCES

Objectives:

To have a Human Resources system based on electronic processes, work-flows and links rather than manual systems and working practices.

To have a fully integrated HR & payroll system.

To ensure that there is only one source of Human Resources information

To provide comprehensive enquiry facilities through a web browser, making it easy for staff to access information on an ad-hoc basis

To ensure the transfer of information into other systems, with audit trails and control reports.

To ensure data is held in a form that can easily be extracted and summarised

To archive data in years and months to provide transaction history

To classify data and the period to be held for before archiving or destruction

To ensure all information has audit trails to origins, amendments and deletions

To allow the import of career and personal history from current system extending back to YEAR

The specified modules are:

  5.1.1   Personnel Management

  5.1.2   Absence

5.1.3   Recruitment

5.1.4   Training

5.1.5   Self Service

5.1.6   Report Writer

5.1.1   Personnel Management

This should contain employee information relating to Personal, Job, Cost Centre, Compensation and Equality.

This data is to be kept relationally, enabling the application to draw comparisons between the attributes for both Person and Post and report on them, e.g.

Headcount: Budget to Actual, the difference being accounted for by vacant posts;

The database should be flexible enough to accommodate multi-posts, where one employee can occupy more than one role, not necessarily in the same grade, and this should accurately be reflected in reporting and organisational structure.

The following features are required:

- Personnel Data which is held only once and accessible from each relevant application module (Please provide details of the data that the system can hold)

- Capability to add extra user define data fields, these data fields to be incorporated into standard enquiries and linked to the self-service module. Please provide details of how this can be done, any related costs and any upgrade implications

- Organisation Chart Management: History and Management

- Rota facilities including monitoring against agreed staffing levels if required

- Bank holidays and ability to consider part time staff work patterns

- Configure work patterns and shift working with regard to sickness, absence and holidays

- Leave recording and authorisation facility

- Equal Opportunities reporting with user defined options to allow for regulatory requirements

- Discipline and Grievance

- Accident Reporting

- Ability to record details of Job Evaluations

- Ability to record staff on Secondment.

- Automatic notification of starters and leavers to key contacts.

- Remind managers of forthcoming retirements via email prompts

- Appraisal, 1-1 Records and competency system – online appraisal (storage and preparation) with facility for employee to confirm Appraisal interviews have taken place and HR to report on Appraisal position across the business

- Legal requirements such as police checks with expiry dates being alerted. Police checks to include CRB checks including reminding staff for CRB checks via email prompts

- Personal Safety Records

- Recording of Child care voucher scheme

- Health and Safety Reporting including accidents and incidents for all staff

- Post identification for Succession Planning.

- Ability to log Occupational Health Referrals on staff details.

- Ability to hold details of different terms and conditions for individual staff members, including variable pay schemes.

- Ability to update salary for various schemes on group basis

- Ability to hold details such as honoraria, acting up allowance, market factors or others with amounts paid under such schemes

- A "menu" system of variable benefits such as flexitime etc. Staff may have a wide range of benefits which may vary over time e.g. luncheon voucher scheme

-

- System must have ability to allow for transfer of as much historical information from legacy systems as possible.

- System should allow for modelling of pay increase either globally or by group members or by different staff groups and within different pay systems e.g. scale and spot

- Ability to monitor against relevant legislative requirements such as the European Working Time directive

- Remind staff for probation period checks via email prompts

- Manage maternity procedures through system prompts

- Manage sickness procedures through system prompts

- Maintain temporary contract staff information

- The capacity to have two jobholders in the same post, e.g. job shares

- The capacity to have one jobholder in 2 part time posts.

- Automatic links to MS Outlook for scheduling tasks for both HR staff and other users

5.1.2   Absence

The following features are required:

Must be able to hold different working patterns and be configurable for part time/ shift working, holidays, Bank holidays and other Council rules, as well as allow for different leave and absence structures, including both non standard hours and part-time leave structures (to be able to calculate leave and absence for different working patterns)

It should also capture detailed Sickness, Maternity/ Paternity/Adoption Leave.

Give real-time update availability for Leave outstanding for any employee, taking account of employees who join or leave during the year requiring pro rata entitlement calculation.

The ability to trigger alerts for long term sickness, expiry of statutory and occupational sick pay, as well as client-determined trends.

Absence recording to include individual occupational health developments.

Absence Reporting including maternity, sickness and annual leave including maintaining totals (time & monetary if possible) of accrued leave carried over from one year to the next.

The absence module should electronically manage, sickness notification forms, self-certification

The absence module must alert users to impending key dates such as, transfer to half pay and GP letters due

5.1.3 Recruitment

The following features are required:

- Must hold complete transaction record or recruitment history, process and package.

- The recruitment module must manage the full term of the vacancy

- Beginning with resignation

- Exit interviews both by reason for leaving and any exit interviews, including confidential information

- Reassessment of posts, including new job descriptions, other post changes and presentation to boards for these changes

- The ability to create a post number at the start of the recruitment process

- Recruitment should integrate with recruitment agencies used, web based and paper based job applications

- A single applicant database should be used for all activities during the recruitment process, short listing, letters for interviews and all other applicant co-ordination

- Applicants based information should, on appointment, create staff records for the appointee

- On-line application facility within system, feeding to our intranet as part of recruitment process

- Ability to attach multiple format documents to any recruitment campaign (e.g. j job adverts produced by third parties)

- Offers/Contracts/Medicals/CRB/ISA's

- Disability checks at the point of recruitment

- Job Profiles including competencies

- User definable electronic application forms

- Ability to number and sort application forms and letters as required against system records of applicant

- Temporary Recruitment – prompts on how long temps have been in post (albeit they are employed by agency. Temporary staff (Agency) should not be part of the establishment, associated reports and not be linked to the payroll

- References (Letters, Documents, and Probationary Periods etc.)

- Maintain all letters, references and application forms

- For both starters and leavers: an audit trail and check list is required of the recruitment process and showing the workflow. This could be used as a tick list to ensure completeness

- Record the details of the standard assessments undertaken for each post as part of the recruitment process. These assessments will be used for future recruitment to that post. The details could be in the form of text and/or attached documents

- Suppliers should list the automatic functionality of the package once a probationary period is completed

- The ability to retain applicant details for a period and to optionally purge those details from the system at user specified intervals.

5.1.4 Training

The following features are required:

- The training module must fully integrate with all appropriate HR and Payroll Modules. Suppliers should state how this is achieved

- The system should hold the training needs assessment and plans at corporate and departmental level. In addition information is required about the budget, actual costs and the officer responsible

- The system should hold the training budget, commitments, plans and actuals for all training and drill down to Corporate and Department levels

- The training must operate on an online basis, that is training programmes should be generated from a person's job / qualifications profile and continually be updated based on relevant activity, including job change, repeat training requirements, health and safety and other courses attended

- The training module should include induction programmes

- Ability to record Post Entry Training funding agreements between Client and employees

- Individual training programmes should provide relevant information to the appraisal process

- The training module should also incorporate a training booking system

- Individual training programmes should contribute to departmental and corporate training plans, including budget and actual costing

- Contain a database of training suppliers containing, type of training provided, course dates and costs

- The training module should also hold previous course material

- Training module should hold the corporate and departmental training plan and budget. There should be automatic updating of delivery against plan.

- Training module to enable actual evaluation of training and evaluation reporting to be undertaken

- Monthly reports on training booked, attended and evaluated for purpose of monitoring

- Remind staff for periodic training via email prompts, i.e. first aider training

- Remind staff that a certification is about to expire to enable refresher training to be organised, i.e. First Aid certificate reminder one month before expiry date.

- Manage all training and development requirements, including TNA and training records

5.1.5 Self Service

This is key element of the new system. The self-service module should be accessible by all staff who can view and control their own personal data with managers being able to view/amend/authorise their staff's information. Verification of the information changes should be carried out by a mixture of managers and Payroll/HR staff. All access to be regulated by configurable security access levels.

Types of personal data to be accessible are shown below;

- Annual Leave

- Sick Leave

- Self certification

- Next of Kin / Emergency contact

- Address

- Bank details

- Updating skills set, i.e. languages spoken, qualifications

- Updating additional info

- Manage expenses online – e.g. travel

- Salary information – e.g. E-payslips

- Pension information

- Staff benefits including credit cards, mobile, cars, laptops, child-care, eye care vouchers

The self-service module should be integrated as much as possible into Microsoft Outlook, so that when staff book leave on the self-service system, it automatically sends them an appointment to populate their Calendar.

The self-service module needs to preferably have a Web Browser front end or if not a Windows-based front end.

5.1.6 Reporting

The following features are required:

- There should be a standard suite of configured reports, which can be varied on an ad hoc basis according to business need.

- Ability to change presentation of reports for easier comprehension.

- A report scheduler that can automate running and distribution (e.g. by emailing recipients) of regular reports.

- User defined enquiries using parameters

- Ability to drill down to get at the source transactions or data

- Tabular and graphical reporting showing trends over prior months/ years.

- Management reporting based on sickness, absence and staff turn-over

- Ability to report retrospectively on information that is held in the system, e.g. to show to show a position that existed at some speci-fied time in the past, up to 7 years.

- The report catalogue must be fully integrated with the fields used in the core HR module and any changes automatically populated to the catalogue to ensure complete reporting. If the report writer is not native to the main HR application, it is required that upgraded versions are joined seamlessly.

5.2 PAYROLL

The Payroll module will be compliant with the fully full range of statutory re-quirements of the HM Revenue & Customs (HMRC), for tax calculations, re-porting, accounting, and exchange of information with employees/ HMRC (e.g. Electronic Data Submission), including production/ printing of P45s, P60s, and Annual Returns.

The module will also and enable full management of Client's payroll opera-tion, handling data capture, processing, printing, distribution and reporting in accordance with the requirements as shown below, and the

5.2.1   System Requirements

In addition to the statutory requirements of a payroll system, the package must also have the capability to be able to:

- Be integrated seamlessly with the other HR modules

- Interface (or export data) to other applications e.g. financials ledger/ MS Office products, Business Objects reporting tool

- Produce Monthly payroll for employees

- Handle pay awards (annual/ multi-year etc.) – with ability for calculating back-pay entitlements

- Manage different contracted hours/ shift patterns

- Ensure system can manage "zero" hour workers e.g. standby, relief staff

- Manage multiple jobs (Including different pay rates, pension contributions, and costing analysis)

- Produce Budget preparation/ forecasting capability either within module or via export of data to other applications e.g. Excel Spreadsheet

- Produce full payroll accounting and gross pay/ costing analysis – monthly totals, cumulative to date, year end, etc. (Standard and ad hoc/ exception reporting)

- Fully compliant with Client requirements for calculations – including banded employee contributions, reporting, accounting and exchange of information with employees/ Pension Fund Administrator.

- Handle arrangements for making payroll deductions for different organisations, e.g. union and social club subscriptions, Child Support Agency, life assurance, etc.

- Expenses payment and related tax reporting (PIID), car mileage / allowances.

- Client Statutory & Occupational Sick pay

- Client Statutory and Occupational Maternity and Paternity Pay

- Ability to deal with Salary sacrifice scheme

- Printing to pre-printed stationery

- To facilitate payslip distribution via electronic methods to all or some employees via self service functionality.

- Compliance with Client general ledger coding rules and budget/ accounting analysis

- Ability to run test payrolls before finalising the payroll for any particular month.

- Run a "standard" monthly payroll (with no temporary input) for business continuity in absence of key staff

- Make single payment runs/ reversals

- Process BACS output/ transmission

- Ability to make manual adjustments to system tax calculations

- Pre-determine tax deductions

- Reverse whole or part pay-runs

- Produce payment controls – cheque/ BACS listing and RTI reporting

- Produce Audit reports – e.g. payroll discrepancy and tolerance reports, payroll deviation reports, exceptions etc.

- Facilitate and record auto-enrolment procedures

5.2.2. Pay, Deduction and Charge Elements

There will be a requirement for the above elements to have scope for expansion.

Typical **Pay** elements will be used for:

- Permanent and temporary

- Taxable and non-taxable

- NI'able and non-ni'able

- Pensionable and non-pensionable

- Various calculation methods (percent, cash, user-defined formulae, rates, multiple of salary)

- Maintaining increasing and decreasing balances

- Mileage payments in according to local scales with correct calculation of tax and national insurance liability

- Automated pay calculation of pay grade increases and allocate back-pay settlements

Typical **Deduction** elements will be used for:

- Permanent and temporary

- Taxable and non-taxable

- Pre or Post Tax

- Pre or Post NI

- User defined arithmetic and conditional calculations

- Maintaining increasing and decreasing balances

Typical **Charge** elements will be used for user defined charge elements that do not form part of pay:

- Permanent and temporary

- Costing purposes when required

- Taxable and non-taxable

- Pensionable and non-pensionable

- User defined arithmetic and conditional calculations

- Maintaining increasing and decreasing balances

5.3 Security & Audit

The system should only allow access via unique user ID and password; this information is encrypted, as there may be access via the Internet

Group and individual access rules to apply to ensure efficient setting up of new users. Please provide a description of how this works

The system has configurable security to ensure that all Client standards and relevant 'data protection act' rules can be adhered to

All relevant data can be easily compiled in order to comply with Data Protection Acts and Freedom of Information Act Requests.

- System security ensures that, if required, users can only access data pertinent to them (e.g. they should only be able to access staff information that they are authorised to use, etc.). This is relevant across all modules

- User-defined access privilege templates can be set up e.g. access templates for departments

- User access can be restricted or granted on individual features/functions within the system

- The system enforces regular password changes and allows for patterns of passwords to be defined by the system administrator (e.g. must not contain just alpha characters). Passwords can be set to expire after a defined period of time

- Passwords must be a minimum of 6 characters and must include at least one capital letter and one numeric

- Passwords for a user are not able to be repeated within a defined period of time. Passwords should have a forced expiry date, notified to the user in advance. Incorrect password usage is logged, and the system bars a user after a number of unsuccessful tries. The information is recorded by user, terminal, date and time.

- Passwords are not shown on the screen or other output. Passwords are encrypted and access to password tables restricted

- The system holds a full audit history of all transactions carried out on the system including who initiated them, the date they were actioned, any changes (details of data before and after change), source documentation, correspondence etc.

- The system holds a log of who has access to the system, what levels of access are granted and what password security restrictions have been applied

- The system provides for system administrator access to administer all modules

- Variable user status which allow self service facilities of all employees and manager input and authorisation for some activity

6. SUPPLIER INFORMATION REQUIRED

Responses to this invitation should be detailed in the following various sections:

6.1 General Information

This should comprise:

- A brief history of the organisation.

- Details of any ultimate Holding Company or Investment backing;

- Addresses of its Registered Office and other business premises;

- Organisational chart;

- Contact details for all respondent's employees to be associated with the contract;

- Web address;

- Name and address of Bankers

- Copies of published and audited accounts for the past three financial years, together with Directors' Reports.

6.2 Application Features

Addressing the Client's outlined requirements on a point by point basis, detailing how the respondent's service will meet those requirements. Where there is non-correspondence, the extent of the discrepancy should be detailed together with any suggested remedy if feasible.

6.3 Technical Specification

A detailed overview of the application's technical configuration and requirements, including

- Platform
- Hardware
- Software
- Broadband capacity
- System performance
- Technical knowledge required and any other relevant factors.

Highlight all areas where the current technical environment as outlined in **3.1** and following does not correspond or may need to be reviewed in the light of the respondent's application requirements.

6.4 Cost

Supply a schedule with each module or stage clearly itemised and accompanied by price indicators as follows:

- Licences
- Software (including third party applications)
- Possible Customisation
- Supplementary Hardware
- Set-Up Costs
- Data Migration
- Consultancy
- Project Management
- System Maintenance
- User Training
- Support Level Options
- Interface to General Ledger
- Any Other Recurring or Non-Recurring Charges

6.5 Implementation

A specimen Project Plan with time scales should accompany the tender document, together with details of:

- Implementation approach and project management methodology to be deployed;

- Quality Assurance standards, approach and any quality accreditations;

- How the respondent's Project personnel will interact with Client project personnel, taking into account their various roles and responsibilities;

- An appreciation of resources, both persons and other physical assets that will be required by Client to perform their part of the project;

- Contingency planning in the event of project setback.

6.6 Evidence of Capacity to Deliver Contract Requirements

Provision of:

- Case studies of the organisation's previous experience of dealing with similar contracts (particular attention should be given to ensure that these studies are relevant, relating to equivalent local authority or public sector clients, and contracts of a similar size).

- Reference sites of comparable sector and size, together with contact details of personnel at those sites.

- Contact details of the application's user group.

- Details of escrow arrangements that may exist in respect of the software;

In the event that sub-contracting likely to be involved, confirmation that the necessary indemnity has been requested and complied with.

6.7 Data Return

In the event of the awarded contract expiring and not being renewed, data will be returned to Client in an acceptable format of their choosing, to be mutually agreed.

6.8 Terms & Conditions

A copy of the organisation's standard trading terms and conditions should accompany the response to this invitation.

6.9 Service Level Agreement

A draft service level agreement, covering administrational operational and other services to be provided by the tendering organisation to Client must be submitted with the response to this Invitation.

MANAGEMENT OF THE TENDER PROCESS

7.1 Delivery of Tenders

Four (4) paper copies and one (1) electronic copy (define medium) of the tender are required. Responses to the invitation must be delivered in a sealed envelope marked "Tender for HR & payroll System" with the tenderer's name and address on the outside.

The tender must be addressed and delivered to:

- Name

- Address

- to arrive not later than **xx hrs. (xx a.m./p.m)** local time on day/ month/year.

- Tenders that are delivered late will be returned unopened.

7.2   Opening of Tenders

Tenders will be opened at **xx hours on date / year**. Only Client personnel assigned to this procurement process will be present at the opening of tenders.

7.3   Timescales

Activity	Time/Date
Date of Notice of Request for Tender	

Final time and date for submission of queries/clarification requests	
Final time and date for receipt of tenders	
Provider Presentations	
Award of Contract	

7.4   Queries about this tender document

Queries regarding this document may be made by fax or by email and must be addressed only to the following:

- Name

- Fax No:

- Email

Tenderers must <u>not</u> contact or discuss this Invitation with any other persons in the Client

Telephone queries will not be taken.

The Client will respond to all queries within (timescale)

7.5   Appendices

Appendices can be included in your Invitation to Tender. Examples can include: Glossary of Terms, Process Diagrams, Interfaces, Strategy Documents, etc.

There should be specimen policies, where available, that are currently in force within the Respondent's organisation relating to Equal Opportunities, Diversity and Sustainability.

7.6   Selection Criteria

This contract will be awarded on criteria agreed by the relevant authorised Client personnel which may reflect functionality, support service, quality assurance, running costs, technical merit, relevant client experience, delivery timetable, and any other relevant matters.

This Invitation to Tender is a request, and does not form a binding contract, nor does it imply any contractual obligation by the Client to any respondent. Tenderers will not be reimbursed for any expenses incurred in the preparation and submission of tenders.

APPENDIX TWO

Sample process map dealing with a Leaver process:

Stage	Action	Responsibility	Date required
	Letter of resignation received, employee leaves in 4 weeks		
1	Letter of acknowledgement together with: • Amount of pro rata holiday entitlement to be liquidated Request to return relevant company property to stated departments: • Car (if applicable) • Laptop /Mobile phone • Other company property • Security card	HR	Immediate response
2.	Leaver form raised and processed	HR & payroll	Immediate
3.	Advise following of termination on date + four weeks: • Medical insurer • Pensions provider • Salary Continuation insurer	HR	Immediate
4	Advise IT to close security access for employee	HR	Final day
5	Advise switchboard to erase employee from list	HR	Final day
6	Manager or relevant person to schedule exit interview	HR	Before final day
7	Advise manager to initiate recruitment replacement process if appropriate	HR	Immediate
8	Final payslip and cheque / payment processed	Payroll	Final day
9	P45 processed	Payroll	Final day
10	Absence to date report processed	HR	Final day

Fig.27 Sample Leaver process map

APPENDIX THREE

Supplier demonstrations – Sample scenarios

These are adaptations of scenarios prepared for a product demonstration round. As you will notice, a certain amount of dummy data and rules needs to be sent beforehand so that the potential vendor can set up the case.

Scenario- 1 HR & payroll

Employee A is a new starter at Company B on a salary of £50,000 p.a and paid on the monthly payroll.

Show how the employee would be processed through the system from the first entry on the database until first salary payment. Please include reference to any new starter documentation, and how electronic workflow can streamline this process.

Shortly after he started work, employee A has a week's sickness absence.. Please show us how this would be recorded on the system using self-service and any associated sickness absence reporting and monitoring. Sickness absence is unpaid for the first three months, so show how this would appear on a payslip.

Employee A transfers from full time to part time working (from 35 hours to 17.5 hours per week). Please show how this is recorded in the HR system, and how holiday entitlements are also changed.

In June, employee A receives a pay award of 5% back-dated to the previous January 1st. Show how this is processed through HR, and how this will show on the payroll and payroll outputs.

After two years, employee A resigns from the company, with one week's annual leave outstanding which is agreed to be liquidated. Please demonstrate the leaver process and how the leave payment would be calculated and paid."

Scenario 2 – Payroll

Employee A is on maternity leave on 30th June and has a pay increase of 3% backdated to April. Show how this can be processed, along with any pension adjustments (according to organisational policy)

Scenario 3 – Payroll

Employee B leaves on January 30 but re-joins the organisation on 3rd.July. Show how this is processed on the payroll.

Scenario 4 – HR

Compile a post profile of Grade C manager Headcount 1.0 FTE, Hours per week: 35; Salary range £35-45,000 non-contributory Medical insurance, 4 x Salary Life assurance, Company Pension scheme A (5% of gross basic salary contribution) Company car grade D.

Attach a new employee to this profile with a salary of £32,500 who is contracted for 30 hours per week.

Scenario 5 – Reporting

Assemble and run a sample report using dummy data provided -showing all stages from scratch-for the following:

Sickness Absence of >3 days between 2 given dates, arranged by department showing employee number, name (in surname order) and duration of absence. Add a calculation to show cost of this absence in terms of annual salary.

Headcount showing budget to actual, calculating total FTE difference to budget and value.

Scenario 6 - Workflow

Compile a workflow process to:

Move a recruitment replacement request document via Self-service from an initiating manager to their divisional head; on approval, that document will be passed to the Financial Accountant for verification of headcount and salary budget and returned to the initiating manager, who then forwards the document to the head of recruitment.

APPENDIX FOUR

THE BIG FIVE BENEFITS OF AN HR SYSTEM

#1: Notifications

a) Actual conversation:

Manager to HR Manager: "It must be coming up for Smith's three-month probation soon"

HR Manager: "Let me check"

A while later, HR Manager: "Actually the date passed 10 days ago. For some reason it didn't get picked up in the diary"

Manager: "Well, not to bother. I've been very busy lately and haven't had a chance to assess him. Let's extend the probation period by a month"

Hard to believe, but I have heard various versions of this over the years. And I have personally experienced something very similar to the following more than a few times.

b) The Marketing Manager who had to use one of the meeting rooms as an office, because no one had advised the Facilities people that she was coming.

c) The Credit Controller who couldn't access the accounts payable system because the computer department hadn't set up a system ID for him.

All the above have two very important issues in common; first, that diary and other informal "reminder" systems are very prone to letting things fall down between the cracks, and secondly, the initial experiences of the new recruits can be described as nothing short of dire. After going through the hoops and expense of identifying and selecting these future stars, the employer has now totally given out the wrong welcoming message.

The simple solution to all these headaches is to be found in your HR system, in the form of what are known as Automatic Trigger or Notifications. This feature can generate an email, system message or SMS in response to changes in data.

A typical example would be when a new employee is entered on the HR database prior to their start date, the configured notification would generate a series of alerts to:

- Advise Security & Switchboard of the arriving newcomer, name, position and department;

- Advise the computer department to create an ID and login;

- Advise the Office Manager of the establishment requirement, as well as provision of car, mobile phone, laptop, where appropriate;

- Later on, at a specified time, e.g. 2 weeks before probation end, advise both starter and hiring manager that there needs to be an assessment on the due date.

We can see that this small adjustment can mean a world of difference to someone in their first days with the organisation, or The Employee Experience as it is now termed. You can go even further with your notifications if you wish: advising your pension providers, medical insurers, and the payroll department if your system is not integrated.

I am a great fan of Notifications, and count them among my Big Five benefits of an HR system as not only do they streamline administration but also go a long way towards suppressing errors and oversights. Look again at your on boarding processes from a new starter point of view, and use your technology to make those important first Impressions favourable and lasting.

#2: Organisation charts

I was visiting a client recently, and found she was busy on a phone call. Whilst waiting in her ante-room, I noticed her secretary frowning at her laptop and sighing.

After a while, I asked her what the problem was. I had opened a floodgate.

"It's these org charts" she said "they're just so fiddly to do, and they change so quickly!" She explained that each department produced their own chart, which was then sent to HR for production of the master chart.

I commiserated, and after my discussion with the client, I asked about the importance of organisation charts to her company. She explained that although it was useful to have a visual representation of the structure, they were of operational value for employee orientation in the on boarding process as well as the strategic benefits of 'at a glance' succession plan and span of control reviews.

Unfortunately, she explained, they had gone back to manual methods after buying some charting software a few years back which had proved unwieldy to use.

This is fairly representative of what I have encountered: the labour-intensive production of charts de-centralised to individual departments, in varying formats such as Excel and Visio and all the results fired at HR for the thankless task of merging. And, of course, while all that is being done, changes in personnel are occurring, so the chart immediately becomes outdated.

Nowadays, enterprises don't always follow the old hierarchical rules as flatter structures and matrix project teams become the norm in certain sectors, but the right HR software can provide accurate real-time charts to those who need them with much less effort. As they are directly linked to the data in the system, they are not only timely, but also factual. The option to have additional flexibility to insert non-standard reporting lines for a true representation is an extra benefit.

Credibility in the HR system and its output are vital for the department and its standing. Equally importantly, the amount of time saved is significant; our consultancy calculated that the equivalent of 1.5 full-time employees would be saved over a 5-year period in a typical enterprise of 1000 employees using manual methods[*].

Don't forget the everlasting gratitude of all involved in the production of manual charts!

#3: Work flow

One of the things I'll never understand is why many organisations create an

---

[*]   *Derived from empirical studies by HRmeansbusiness Ltd over a rolling 10 year period). Copyright ©HRmeansbusiness Ltd 2018*

obstacle course for hiring managers when there's a need to recruit a replacement employee.

Typically, a requisition is raised, passed to the next manager up the food chain, then to the Finance head, then to HR and finally to the CEO. Apart from the "trust your managers" issue, the delays caused by this largely unnecessary paper trail percolating through several in-trays can cause a large hole in departmental performance.

To show the flip side of the same problem, I recall a case, where the Managing Director needed a new head of Marketing. He knew who he wanted, took them out to lunch and clinched the deal. Due to sickness and holidays, the unfortunate HR department took nearly three months to secure the necessary authorisations a posteriori for the file.

Well, even if your business wants to keep this unwieldy process going, work flow can take the legwork out of authorisation without moving any paper around.

This works by setting up and selecting a standard document in your HR self service module which is then completed by the initiating party and routed by a pre-configured protocol for approval. At each stage, the document does not move until the correct approval has been secured.

So what's different? Recipients see this appearing in their inbox with increasing frequency and / or level of priority, which encourages action. Nothing is buried under a mound of other papers while someone is away or sick. Authorisation is simple, being a matter of one or two clicks, and the request continues on its journey.

I always urge clients to overhaul their key processes before committing to implement a new system, as it's a great chance to sweep away irrelevancies. But to set up effective work flow, you need to invest time and effort to get it right, and test for illogical elements; one Chief Executive I knew came back from a long business trip to find her inbox chock-full of holiday and sickness forms for approval. Why? Because default approvers had not been written in correctly for absent managers, and tasks that could not be find authorisation automatically escalated upwards!

Work flow can also be applied to many areas of the business where approval processes are needed, such a staff benefits changes, sickness absence and development needs that have been identified by reviews, as well as the reviews themselves.

Training sessions on the new software is the ideal time to learn to construct these processes, starting with basic ones and then more complex ones can be structured as user confidence grows.

Our consultancy reckons in a typical organisation of 1000 employees, work flow saves about 1.25 FTE of time, and that is a very conservative figure, as it does not factor in the reduction in time to hire* Work flow certainly merits its place on the Big Five Benefits podium.

#4: Self service

Every HR person will know the frustration of being interrupted by a phone call or visit from an employee to find out how much holiday they have left.

An employee complains that their salary has gone into their old bank account. The Change form is found not to have been processed.

I've seen many HR offices with a 'Twilight Zone' where self-certification sickness forms lie fallow until an overworked HR assistant is despatched to clear some of them.

What do these three commonplace problems have in common? The first is a waste of two people's time, the second is a nuisance for the employee and the third guarantees that any management figures on absence are inaccurate.

They can all be cured by the self service module in an HR system.

Self service has come a long way since its inception when it was both costly and limited in its uses; an additional downside was that the systems were run on in-house servers, and so to use self service one would have to be on the company premises unless you had grudgingly-granted remote access rights.

These days, self service is a standard feature of mainstream HR software and gives appropriate access to all who need to view or take action. Employees can view their personal records and have the facility to change or modify certain fields such as Address, Bank Details or Emergency Contact, as well as generate requests for Holidays, Training or submit Sickness absence data. Managers can view their departmental data as well as standard or bespoke reports at any time; many HR colleagues tell me that they do their analyses on the train home!

Self service also enables actions such as appraisal reporting online, connecting it to objective setting and consequent training / developmental needs; these in turn can be approved and booked using work flow deployed through the module.

Don't underestimate the amount of preparation for all this, as there are varying security layers to configure for every employee. Additionally, this represents a significant culture change for any organisation, so time and resources must be invested in gaining acceptance and giving user training; don't assume everyone will take to it like a duck to water.

The HRmeansbusiness consultancy has calculated that a typical organisation of 1000 employees, saves round 5 FTE of time over a 5 year period, and that is conservative figure*. The greater part of time and admin. saving will be made in HR activity, but a bigger advantage is making data available effectively in real time, which makes the Self Service business case irresistible.

#5: Report writer

Could you figure in headlines like "Employers 'named and shamed' over minimum wage failings" (There were some household names in there)?

Are you confident about meeting your statutory obligations with compulsory gender pay gap submissions (lots of companies aren't)

Are you committed to providing managerial and operational staff with the information they need?

These and similar questions are causing considerable corporate unease; if the big guns can't get it right, how are we going to cope?

Actually, it shouldn't be a problem at all if you use your HR system's report writer to do the hard work for you.

Let's go right back to the beginning. The data you put into your system must be accurate. Seems, obvious, doesn't it, but I can safely say the majority of my clients have said at the outset that they consider their data as "iffy", "mainly correct" or somewhere in between..

Self service makes employees responsible for much of their data, but there needs to be a rigorous control procedure in place that dictates that changes authorised by managers such as salary, position, department and so on must be reflected in the system by them without exception. HR people have wasted enough time chasing omissions and oversights by operational managers.

Secondly, the data must be timely. If your absence or performance stats are a month out of date, then the output is only fit for historical purposes, which in this era of lightning change is fairly irrelevant. Wide-ranging self service rights eliminate the old problem of paper holiday requests or sickness absence forms piling up in the HR office.

Next, the right reports need to be configured. In times gone by, HR system report writers were ponderous and needed a degree in logic to master, but now they are much more intuitive and user-friendly. Work out what the desired report should reflect and how it should appear, identify the data elements, and use filters and other qualifying tools to arrive at the desired result. You may have to experiment at first to get what you are looking for. I would commend to any practitioner that they invest time and resource in getting proficient in this vital part of the software. The ability to present data in required formats is now an essential part of any HR professional's job.

The reports that you and your organisation need will be driven by

a) compliance, such as determining gender pay gap, equal opportunities monitoring, eligibility to work and testing for minimum wage legislation adherence;

b) financial, examples being headcount and salary budgets to actual;

c) effectiveness monitoring, such as tracking effectiveness of your learning / training outgoings by looking at performance improvement after the event and

d) general management and operational, showing areas of absence, poor performance or employee attrition that could signal local manager problems.

These are just some examples of the types of reports you'll need to be able to configure in your system. The content of b, c and d will vary from enterprise to enterprise, and here is where you need to be in close communication with those departments (your internal clients) to establish exactly what information they need, and what your system can offer them. Being proactive at this point will help your cause immensely.

If you need help with compiling the report structure, don't hesitate to contact your HR system supplier; they will give you the very best advice, and may even have a template that you can modify to save time.

Finally: remember that these reports are of vital importance to your organisation. Don't be a gatekeeper. Make them freely available to your key players via the self service system. This is one of the best ways to demonstrate HR's true value.

www.ingramcontent.com/pod-product-compliance
Lightning Source LLC
Chambersburg PA
CBHW060301220326
41598CB00027B/4193